Cures for Love

D0768026

STENDHAL

Cures for Love

Translated into English prose by
GILBERT *and* SUZANNE SALE

GREAT 🐧🐧 LOVES

PENGUIN BOOKS

Published by the Penguin Group
Penguin Books Ltd, 80 Strand, London WC2R 0RL, England
Penguin Group (USA) Inc., 375 Hudson Street, New York, New York 10014, USA
Penguin Group (Canada), 90 Eglinton Avenue East, Suite 700, Toronto, Ontario, Canada M4P 2Y3
(a division of Pearson Penguin Canada Inc.)
Penguin Ireland, 25 St Stephen's Green, Dublin 2, Ireland
(a division of Penguin Books Ltd)
Penguin Group (Australia), 250 Camberwell Road, Camberwell, Victoria 3124, Australia
(a division of Pearson Australia Group Pty Ltd)
Penguin Books India Pvt Ltd, 11 Community Centre, Panchsheel Park, New Delhi – 110 017, India
Penguin Group (NZ), 67 Apollo Drive, Rosedale, North Shore 0632, New Zealand
(a division of Pearson New Zealand Ltd)
Penguin Books (South Africa) (Pty) Ltd, 24 Sturdee Avenue,
Rosebank, Johannesburg 2196, South Africa

Penguin Books Ltd, Registered Offices: 80 Strand, London WC2R 0RL, England

www.penguin.com

This translation published by The Merlin Press 1957
Published in Penguin Books 1957
This extract published in Penguin Books 2007

1

Translation copyright © The Merlin Press, 1957
All rights reserved

Typeset by Rowland Phototypesetting Ltd, Bury St Edmunds, Suffolk
Printed in England by Clays Ltd, St Ives plc

Except in the United States of America, this book is sold subject
to the condition that it shall not, by way of trade or otherwise, be lent,
re-sold, hired out, or otherwise circulated without the publisher's
prior consent in any form of binding or cover other than that in
which it is published and without a similar condition including this
condition being imposed on the subsequent purchaser

978-0-141-03477-5

Contents

Marie Henri Beyle, known through his writings as Stendhal (1783–1842) was born in Grenoble, France. A cousin offered him a post in the Ministry of War and from 1800 onwards he followed Napoleon's campaigns in Italy, Germany, Russia and Austria. After the fall of Napoleon he retired to Italy, adopted his pseudonym, and started to write books on Italian painting, Haydn and Mozart, and travels in Italy. In 1818, when he was in his mid-thirties, Stendhal met and fell passionately in love with the beautiful Mathilde Dembowski. She, however, was quick to make it clear that she did not return his affections, and in his despair he turned to the written word to exorcise his love and explain his feelings. The result was *De l'Amour*, from where these extracts are taken: an intensely personal dissection of the process of falling – and being – in love. This was followed by *Racine et Shakespeare*, a defence of romantic literature and *Le Rouge et le Noir*, his second novel. He also produced or began three others, none of which was received with any great understanding during his lifetime.

CHAPTER I
On Love

I want to try and establish exactly what this passion is, whose every genuine manifestation is characterized by beauty.

There are four different kinds of love:

1. Passionate Love. This was the love of the Portuguese nun, that of Heloïse for Abelard, of the captain of Vésel, and of the gendarme of Cento.

2. Mannered Love, which flourished in Paris about 1760, and which is to be found in the memoirs and novels of the period; for example those of Crébillon, Lauzun, Duclos, Marmontel, Chamfort, and Mme d'Epinay . . .

A stylized painting, this, where the rosy hues extend into the shadows, where there is no place for anything at all unpleasant – for that would be a breach of etiquette, of good taste, of delicacy, and so forth. A man of breeding will know in advance all the rituals he must meet and observe in the various stages of this kind of love, which often achieves greater refinement than real love, since there is nothing passionate or unpredictable about it, and it is always witty. It is a cold, pretty miniature as against an oil painting by one of the Carrachi; and while passionate love carries us away against our real interests, mannered love as invariably respects those interests. Admittedly, if you take away vanity, there is very little left of mannered love, and the poor weakened invalid can hardly drag itself along.

3. Physical Love. You are hunting; you come across a handsome young peasant girl who takes to her heels through the woods. Everyone knows the love that springs from this kind of pleasure, and however desiccated and miserable you may be, this is where your love-life begins at sixteen.

4. Vanity-Love. The great majority of men, especially in France, both desire and possess a fashionable woman, much in the way one might own a fine horse – as a luxury befitting a young man. Vanity, a little flattered and a little piqued, leads to enthusiasm. Sometimes there is physical love, but not always; often even physical pleasure is lacking. 'A duchess is never more than thirty in the eyes of a bourgeois,' said the Duchesse de Chaulnes, and the courtiers of that just king Louis of Holland cheerfully recall even now a pretty woman from The Hague who was quite unable to resist the charms of anyone who happened to be a duke or a prince. But true to hierarchical principles, as soon as a prince came to court she would send her duke packing. She was rather like an emblem of seniority in the diplomatic corps!

The happiest version of this insipid relationship is where physical pleasure grows with habit. Then memories produce a semblance of love; there is the pricking at your pride and the sadness in satisfaction; the atmosphere of romantic fiction catches you by the throat, and you believe yourself lovesick and melancholy, for vanity will always pretend to be grand passion. One thing is certain though: whichever kind of love produces the pleasures, they only become vivid, and their recollection compelling, from the moment of inspiration. In love, unlike most other passions, the recollection of what you have had and lost is always better than what you can hope for in the future.

Occasionally in vanity-love, habit, or despair of finding something better, results in a friendship of the least attractive sort, which will even boast of its *stability*, and so on.

Although physical pleasure, being natural, is known to all, it is only of secondary importance to sensitive, passionate people. If such people are derided in drawing rooms or made unhappy by the intrigues of the worldly, they possess in compensation a knowledge of pleasures utterly inaccessible to those moved only by vanity or money.

Some virtuous and sensitive women are almost unaware of the idea of physical pleasure; they have so rarely, if I may hazard an expression, exposed themselves to it, and in fact the raptures of passionate love have practically effaced the memory of bodily delights.

There are some men who are the victims and instruments of a hellish pride, a pride like that of Alfieri. These men, who are cruel perhaps because like Nero they are always afraid, judge everyone after their own pattern, and can achieve physical pleasure only when they indulge their pride by practising cruelties upon the companion of their pleasures. Hence the horrors of *Justine*. Only in this way can they find a sense of security.

Instead of defining four kinds of love, one might well admit eight or ten distinctions. There are perhaps as many different ways of feeling as there are of seeing, but differences of terminology do not affect the arguments which follow. Every variety of love mentioned henceforth is born, lives, dies, or attains immortality in accordance with the same laws.

CHAPTER 2
The Birth of Love

Here is what happens in the soul:

1. Admiration.

2. You think, 'How delightful it would be to kiss her, to be kissed by her,' and so on . . .

3. Hope. You observe her perfections, and it is at this moment that a woman really ought to surrender, for the utmost physical pleasure. Even the most reserved women blush to the whites of their eyes at this moment of hope. The passion is so strong, and the pleasure so sharp, that they betray themselves unmistakably.

4. Love is born. To love is to enjoy seeing, touching, and sensing with all the senses, as closely as possible, a lovable object which loves in return.

5. The first crystallization begins. If you are sure that a woman loves you, it is a pleasure to endow her with a thousand perfections and to count your blessings with infinite satisfaction. In the end you overrate wildly, and regard her as something fallen from Heaven, unknown as yet, but certain to be yours.

Leave a lover with his thoughts for twenty-four hours, and this is what will happen:

At the salt mines of Salzburg, they throw a leafless

5

wintry bough into one of the abandoned workings. Two or three months later they haul it out covered with a shining deposit of crystals. The smallest twig, no bigger than a tom-tit's claw, is studded with a galaxy of scintillating diamonds. The original branch is no longer recognizable.

What I have called crystallization is a mental process which draws from everything that happens new proofs of the perfection of the loved one.

You hear a traveller speaking of the cool orange groves beside the sea at Genoa in the summer heat: Oh, if you could only share that coolness with *her*!

One of your friends goes hunting, and breaks his arm: wouldn't it be wonderful to be looked after by the woman you love! To be with her all the time and to see her loving you . . . a broken arm would be heaven . . . and so your friend's injury provides you with conclusive proof of the angelic kindness of your mistress. In short, no sooner do you think of a virtue than you detect it in your beloved.

The phenomenon that I have called crystallization springs from Nature, which ordains that we shall feel pleasure and sends the blood to our heads. It also evolves from the feeling that the degree of pleasure is related to the perfections of the loved one, and from the idea that 'She is mine.' The savage has no time to go beyond the first step. He feels pleasure, but his brain is fully occupied in chasing deer through the forest, so that he can eat, keep up his strength, and avoid his enemy's axe.

At the other end of the scale of civilization, I have no doubt that a sensitive woman can feel physical pleasure only with the man she loves. This is the direct opposite of the savage's condition. But then, in civilized countries, the woman has leisure, while the savage is so taken up with his occupation that he cannot help treating his female as a beast of burden. If the mates of many animals are happier, it is only because the male has less difficulty in obtaining his food.

But let us leave the forest and return to Paris. A man in love sees every perfection in the object of his love, but his attention is still liable to wander after a time because one gets tired of anything uniform, even perfect happiness.

This is what happens next to fix the attention:

6. Doubt creeps in. First a dozen or so glances, or some other sequence of actions, raise and confirm the lover's hopes. Then, as he recovers from the initial shock, he grows accustomed to his good fortune, or acts on a theory drawn from the common multitude of easily-won women. He asks for more positive proofs of affection and tries to press his suit further.

He is met with indifference, coldness, or even anger if he appears too confident. In France there is even a shade of irony which seems to say 'You think you're farther ahead than you really are.' A woman may behave like this either because she is recovering from a moment of intoxication and obeying the dictates of modesty, which she may fear she has offended; or simply for the sake of prudence or coquetry.

The lover begins to be less sure of the good fortune he was anticipating and subjects his grounds for hope to a critical examination.

He tries to recoup by indulging in other pleasures but finds them inane. He is seized by the dread of a frightful calamity and now concentrates fully. Thus begins:

7. The second crystallization, which deposits diamond layers of proof that 'she loves me.'

Every few minutes throughout the night which follows the birth of doubt, the lover has a moment of dreadful misgiving, and then reassures himself, 'she loves me'; and crystallization begins to reveal new charms. Then once again the haggard eye of doubt pierces him and he stops transfixed. He forgets to draw breath and mutters, 'But does she love me?' Torn between doubt and delight, the poor lover convinces himself that she could give him such pleasure as he could find nowhere else on earth.

It is the pre-eminence of this truth, and the road to it, with a fearsome precipice on one hand and a view of perfect happiness on the other, which set the second crystallization so far above the first.

The lover's mind vacillates between three ideas:

1. She is perfect.
2. She loves me.
3. How can I get the strongest possible proofs of her love?

The most heartrending moment of love in its infancy is the realization that you have been mistaken about something, and that a whole framework of crystals has to be destroyed. You begin to feel doubtful about the entire process of crystallization.

CHAPTER 3
The Different Beginnings of Love for the Two Sexes

A woman establishes her position by granting favours. Ninety-five per cent of her daydreams are about love, and from the moment of intimacy they revolve about one single theme: she endeavours to justify the extraordinary and decisive step she has taken in defiance of all her habits of modesty. A man has no such concern, but a woman's imagination dwells reminiscently on every enchanting detail.

Since love casts doubt upon what seemed proven before, the woman who was so certain, before intimacy, that her lover was entirely above vulgar promiscuity, no sooner remembers that she has nothing left to refuse him than she trembles lest he has merely been adding another conquest to his list.

Only at this point does the second crystallization begin, and much more strongly, since it is now accompanied by fear.

The woman feels she has demeaned herself from queen to slave, and matters are aggravated by the dizzy intoxication which results from pleasures as keen as they are rare. And then again, a woman at her embroidery – an insipid pastime that occupies only her hands – thinks of nothing but her lover; while he, galloping

9

across the plains with his squadron, would be placed under arrest if he muffed a manœuvre.

I should imagine, therefore, that the second crystallization is a good deal stronger in women, because fear is more acute; vanity and honour are in pawn and distractions are certainly not so easy.

A woman cannot fall back on the habit of rational thinking that a man like myself is bound to acquire, working six hours a day at a desk on cold rational matters. Women are inclined, and not only in love, to give way to their imaginations, and to become ecstatic; so their lovers' faults are quickly effaced.

Women prefer emotion to reason. It's quite simple: since in our dull way we never give them any business responsibility in the family *they never have occasion to use reason*, and so never regard it as of any use.

Indeed they find reason a positive nuisance, since it descends upon them only to chide them for their enjoyment of yesterday, or to forbid them the enjoyment of tomorrow.

If you were to hand over the administration of two of your estates to your wife, I wager the accounts would be better kept than by yourself; and then . . . well, you would of course have the *right* to feel sorry for yourself, you pitiable despot, since you lack even the talent to excite love.

As soon as women begin to generalize they are making love without knowing it. They pride themselves on being more meticulous in detail than men, and half the trade across counters is carried on by women, who do better at it than their husbands. It is a commonplace that when you talk about business with them, you must always adopt a very serious tone.

The thing is that they are hungry for emotion, anywhere and at any time: think of the pleasures of a Scottish funeral.

CHAPTER 4

The First Step, High Society, Misfortunes

The most surprising thing of all about love is the first step, the violence of the change that takes place in a man's mind. Society, with its brilliant parties, helps love by making this *first step* easier.

The beginning is the change from simple admiration to tender admiration. (What a pleasure to kiss her . . . etc.)

A whirling waltz in a drawing-room lit by a thousand candles will set young hearts afire, banish shyness, bring a new awareness of strength, and in the end give *the courage to love*. Because in order to fall in love it is not enough just to see a lovely person; on the contrary, extreme loveliness deters the sensitive. You have to see her, if not in love with you, at least stripped of her dignity.

Imagine falling in love with a queen, unless she made the first advances!

The ideal breeding-ground for love is the boredom of solitude, with the occasional long-awaited ball; wise mothers of daughters are guided accordingly.

Genuine 'high society', such as was to be found at the French court, but which I think ceased to exist in 1780, was hardly propitious to the growth of love, since *solitude* and leisure were almost impossible to obtain there, and both of these are necessary for the crystallization process.

Court life trains you to perceive and express a great number of different *shades of meaning*, and a subtly expressed nuance may be the beginning of admiration and then passion.

When love's troubles are mixed with others (those of *vanity*: when your mistress offends your proper pride, your sense of honour or of personal dignity; those of health, money, or political persecution, etc . . .) it is only superficially that love is increased by the difficulties. Since they engage the imagination elsewhere, they prevent the crystallizations of hopeful love and the growth of little doubts in requited love. The sweetness and the madness of love return when these difficulties are removed.

Note that misfortune favours the birth of love in superficial or unfeeling people. Love is also helped by misfortunes which precede it, for the imagination then recoils from the outside world which offers only sad pictures, and throws itself wholeheartedly into the task of crystallization.

CHAPTER 5
First Sight

Even the most ingenuous women, if they have any imagination, are sensitive and *suspicious*. They may be mistrustful without knowing it; after all, life has been full of disillusionment! So everything formal or commonplace in their first encounter with a man scares their imagination, and the likelihood of crystallization is deferred. In a romantic situation, on the other hand, love conquers at first sight.

The process is simple: you are surprised, and as a result you ponder over the event that surprised you. You are already halfway to the state of mind in which crystallization takes place.

As an example, take the beginning of Seraphine's love affair in the second volume of *Gil Blas*. Don Fernando is describing his flight from the *sbirri* of the Inquisition: 'It was quite dark, and the rain was pelting down; I had crossed several alley-ways and suddenly came upon the open door of a drawing-room. I went in, and at once became aware of the magnificence of the place . . . on one side I saw a door a little ajar. I half opened it and could see a vista of rooms, the last of which was lighted. I wondered what to do next . . . Overcome with curiosity I crept forward through the rooms until I reached the light, which proved to be a candle in a gilt candlestick, standing on a marble table. Then I noticed a bed, whose curtains were partly drawn aside because of the heat, and my attention was riveted by the sight of a young woman who lay asleep, in spite of the thunderclap which had just shaken the house ... I moved a little closer ... I felt overpowered ... While I was standing there, dizzy with the pleasure of looking at her, she awoke ...

'Imagine her surprise at seeing in her room, at dead of night, a man she had never set eyes on before. She gave a great start, and uttered a cry ... I tried to reassure her, and went down on one knee. "Please," I said, "don't be afraid ..." She called to her maids ... A little emboldened by the presence of her little serving-maid, she asked me with spirit who I was ... etc., etc.'

Here is an example of 'first sight' which it is not easy to forget. In contrast, what could be more idiotic than our custom nowadays of introducing a girl to her 'intended', formally and also a trifle sentimentally! Legalized prostitution; a mere mockery of modesty.

Chamfort relates how, on the afternoon of 17th February 1790, he attended a 'family ceremony', as it is called. That is to say, respectable folks, reputedly honest, had gathered together to witness and applaud the happiness of one Mademoiselle de Marille, a lovely, witty, and virtuous young woman, who was being privileged to become the wife of M. R—, an unhealthy, repulsive, doltish, but wealthy old man. She had seen him for the third time that very day at the signing of the contract.

'If anything can be said to characterize this infamous century,' Chamfort continues, 'it is that such a matter should be cause for rejoicing; that joy should be mocked; and, in the long view, that these same people should behave with icy contempt and heartless prudery at the least imprudence of a lovesick young woman.'

Since it is essentially artificial and predetermined, anything which smacks of ceremony or demands *seemly behaviour* paralyses the imagination and allows it to dwell only on the undignified and irrelevant; hence the magical effect of a joke at such a time. The poor girl, painfully shy and modest during the introduction to her future husband, can think only of the part she is playing, and this is another certain way of stifling imagination.

It is a far greater sin against modesty to go to bed with a man only twice seen, after three words of Latin in a church, than to surrender despite oneself to a man adored for two years. But of course I am talking nonsense.

The prolific source of the vice and misery which follow marriage nowadays is Popery. It makes freedom impossible for girls before marriage and divorce impossible afterwards, when they find they have made a mistake – or rather a mistake has been made for them – in the choice of a husband. Look at Germany, that country of happy homes, where that charming princess, Madame la Duchesse de Sagan, has just got most respectably married for the fourth time. What is more, she invited to the wedding her three former husbands, with whom she remains on the best of terms. This is of course overdoing it; but a single divorce that puts paid to a husband's tyrannies can prevent thousands of unhappy homes. The joke of it all is that Rome is one of the places where divorces are most frequent.

A prerequisite of love is that a man's face, at first sight, should reveal something to be respected, and something to be pitied.

CHAPTER 6
Infatuation

High breeding is often marked by curiosity and prejudice, and these ominous symptoms are generally apparent when the sacred flame – the origin of all the passions – has gone out. Schoolboys entering society for the first time are also a prey to infatuation. In youth and age, too many or too few sensibilities prevent one from perceiving things as they really are, and from experiencing the true sensations which they impart.

Some people, over-fervent, or fervent by starts – loving on credit, if I may put it that way – will hurl themselves upon the experience instead of waiting for it to happen. Before the nature of an object can produce its proper sensation in them, they have blindly invested it from afar with imaginary charm which they conjure up inexhaustibly within themselves. As they come closer they see the experience not as it is, but as they have made it. They take delight in their own selves in the mistaken belief that they are enjoying the experience. But sooner or later they get tired of making the running and discover that the object of their adoration is *not returning the ball*; then their infatuation is dispelled, and the slight to their self-respect makes them react unfairly against the thing they once overrated.

CHAPTER 7
The Introduction

I am lost in admiration of the shrewdness and sure judgement with which women grasp certain details. A moment later I see them praising folly, moved to tears by mawkishness, and gravely weighing mere affectation as a trait of character. How they can be so silly is beyond me. There must be some law of nature I haven't heard about.

They concentrate on *one* quality, *one* detail in a man, and are so taken up with it that they have no eyes for the rest. All their nervous fluid is engaged in enjoying this one quality so that there is none to spare for perceiving others.

I have seen really first-rate men being introduced to highly intelligent women, but it is always the same: a trace of prejudice, and the consequences of a first meeting are decided in advance.

Let me be personal for a moment, and I will tell you how the charming colonel La Bédoyère was about to meet Madame Struve from Koenigsberg, a really fine woman. We were all wondering, '*Fara colpo?*' (would she succumb to him?) and a bet was laid. I went to Madame de Struve and told her that the colonel wore his cravats two days running, and turned them inside out on the second day. If she looked, I said, she would notice the vertical creases on his cravat. The whole story was manifestly untrue.

Just as I finished, the good colonel himself was announced. The most insignificant little ass in Paris would have called forth more response from the lady. Mind you, Madame de Struve was in love; she was a sincere person, and there could never have been a light-hearted affair between them.

Never were two characters more fitted for each other. Madame de Struve was accused of being 'romantic', and the only thing that could touch La Bédoyère was virtuousness carried to its most romantic extreme. It was for her sake that he shot himself, while he was still quite young.

Women are very clever at feeling the imperceptible changes in the human heart, and at distinguishing nuances of affection or the least flicker of pride. They have a sense-organ for this, that men have not; watch them tending a wounded man.

But perhaps at the same time they do not see the thing called intelligence, a moral compound. I have seen some of the best women merely passing the time of day with an intelligent man (not myself, by the way) while at the same time, and indeed almost in the same breath, they were lost in the admiration of utter fools. I have stood fascinated, like an expert who sees the finest diamonds mistaken for paste, while paste ones, being larger, are preferred.

I argued from this that where women are concerned one must dare all. Where General Lasalle failed, a captain bristling with oaths and mustachios succeeded. The whole of one side of men's qualities must be completely missed by women.

For my part, I fall back as usual on the laws of physic. The nervous fluid is taken up in men by the brain, and in women by the heart; that's why they are more vulnerable. Men can find consolation in having to get down to some important task in their chosen and accustomed profession; women have nothing to console them but idle distractions.

I was exchanging ideas tonight with Appiani, who believes in virtue only as a last resort. When I expounded the gist of this chapter he said: 'You remember Eponina, who kept her husband alive in an underground cavern so devotedly and heroically? The force of character she showed in keeping up his spirits would have been used to hide a lover from her husband if they had been living quietly in Rome. Strong characters need strong nourishment.'

CHAPTER 8
Glances

Glances are the big guns of the virtuous coquette; everything can be conveyed in a look, and yet that look can always be denied, because it cannot be quoted word for word.

It reminds me of Comte Giraud, the Mirabeau of Rome. Because of the nice little Government of this part of the world he has developed an original method of communication, using amputated words which mean everything and yet nothing. He conveys his meaning amply, but you cannot compromise him, however much you quote him verbatim. Cardinal Lante accused him of having stolen this accomplishment from women; and I would say that even the most honest woman knows the trick. It is a cruel but just reprisal for the tyranny of man.

Everyone must have seen little girls of three very creditably discharging the obligations of gallantry.

Mannered love is stimulated by confidences, while passionate love is cooled by them.

Confidences present difficulties as well as dangers. In passionate love, what you cannot express (because language is too coarse to achieve the required nuance) exists none the less, only it is so fine-drawn that error in observing it is more probable.

And an observer under the stress of emotion observes badly; he fails to give chance her due.

Perhaps the wisest thing is to confide in oneself. Using borrowed names, but including all the relevant details, write down tonight what took place between you and your mistress, and the problems with which you are faced. In a week's time, if you are suffering from passionate love, you will be someone else entirely, and then, on reading your case-history, you will be able to give yourself good advice.

Among men, whenever more than two are gathered together and envy might be aroused, politeness demands that the talk should be confined to physical love. The after-dinner conversation at men's parties is a case in point. Baffo's sonnets are the ones recited, and they give great pleasure, because each person takes his neighbour's praise and enthusiasm literally, though very often the neighbour only wishes to appear gay or polite. French madrigals or the tender charm of Petrarch would be out of place.

CHAPTER 9
Jealousy

When you are in love, no matter what you see or remember, whether you are packed in a gallery listening to political speeches or riding at full gallop under enemy fire to relieve a garrison, you are always adding new perfections to your idea of your mistress, or finding new and apparently ideal ways of making her love you more.

Each step your imagination takes brings a new delight. Little wonder that this state of mind is enticing.

Though the same habit persists, the moment you become jealous it produces an opposite effect. Far from giving you sublime joy, every perfection added into the crown of your beloved, who perhaps loves another, is a dagger-thrust in the heart. 'This delight,' cries a voice, 'is for your rival!'

And when other things strike you, instead of suggesting new ways of increasing her love, they indicate more of your rival's advantages.

You see a pretty woman galloping in the park, and the rival is immediately famed for his fine horses which can take him ten miles in fifty minutes.

This mood can easily turn to fury. You forget that

in love *possession is nothing, only enjoyment matters.* You overrate your rival's success, and the insolence resulting from it. Then you reach the final torment: utter despair poisoned still further by a shred of hope.

Probably the only solution is to observe your rival's good fortune very closely. Often you will find him placidly dozing in the very drawing-room which contains the woman the thought of whom stops your heart beating when you see, far down a street, a hat which might be hers.

If you want him to wake up, just betray your jealousy. You will then perhaps have the privilege of informing him how valuable is this woman who prefers him to you, and you will be the author of his love for her.

Where your rival is concerned there is no middle course; you must either joke with him in the most detached way, or frighten him off.

Since jealousy is the greatest of all ills, you can find a pleasant diversion in risking your life. Because then your thoughts will not be entirely embittered (by the process described above) and you will be able to play with the idea of killing your rival.

On the principle that one should never reinforce the strength of the enemy, you must conceal your love from your rival. Secretly, calmly, and simply, and on some pretext totally unrelated to love, you should say: 'Sir, I do not know why the public chooses to credit me with little Miss So-and-so, and is even so good as to believe me in love with her. If you wanted her, why, you could have her with all my heart, were it not that unfortunately I should be made to look a fool. In six months' time you can have all you want of her, but today the honour, which, heaven knows why, attaches to these things, compels me to warn you, to my great regret, that if by any chance you lack the fairness to await your turn, one of us will have to die.'

Your rival is most probably not a passionate man, and may be a very prudent one. Once he is convinced of your resolve he will hasten to surrender the woman upon the first convenient pretext. This is why your declaration must be made lightheartedly and the whole affair shrouded in the utmost secrecy.

What makes jealousy so painful is that you cannot employ vanity to help you bear it, but the method I have explained gives vanity a clear field. You can admire your own bravery, even if you are inclined to despise yourself as an inspirer of love.

If you would rather not be melodramatic, the best thing to do is travel forty leagues and find a dancer to entertain, whose charms should appear to have halted you as you were passing.

Unless your rival has extraordinary insight, he will think you have got over your passion.

Very often the best plan is to wait impassively until your rival, by his own blunders, wears out his welcome with your beloved. Because, barring the case of a grand passion built up stage by stage in early youth, a woman will not love a fool for long. In the case of jealousy after intimacy, you need both apparent indifference and genuine inconstancy, for many women, merely angry with a man they still love, will attach themselves to a man of whom their lover shows jealousy, until suddenly the game becomes a reality.

I have covered this in some detail because in these moments of jealousy one usually loses one's head, and advice written beforehand is a help. Besides, since the important thing is to pretend to keep calm, it is right and proper to learn the right atmosphere from philosophical writings.

Since you are only vulnerable through the proffer or denial of things whose whole value depends on your passion, by managing to sham indifference you disarm your adversaries at one blow.

If there is no action that can be taken, and you can amuse yourself by seeking solace, you will get some pleasure from reading *Othello*. Even the most damning appearances will be laid open to doubt, and you will pause delightedly over the words:

> *Trifles light as air*
> *Seem to the jealous, confirmations strong*
> *As proofs from holy writ.*
> > *Othello*. Act III

I have found consolation in a beautiful view of the sea.

The morning which had arisen calm and bright, gave a pleasant effect to the waste mountain view which was seen from the castle on looking to the landward; and the glorious Ocean crisped with a thousand rippling waves of silver, extended on the other side in awful yet complacent majesty to the verge of the horizon. With such scenes of calm sublimity, the human heart sympathizes even in HIS most disturbed moods, and deeds of honour and virtue are inspired by their majestic influence.

(*The Bride of Lammermoor.* Vol. 1.)

In one of Salviati's manuscripts I found this: '20th July, 1818. – A little unreasonably, I think, I often apply to life as a whole a feeling comparable to that of an ambitious man or of a good patriot during a battle, when he is detailed to look after reserve stores or ordered to some post away from danger and action. I should have been sorry to reach forty and to be past the age of loving, without having experienced passion deeply. I should have felt the bitter and degrading pain of realizing too late that I had been tricked into letting life go by without living.

'I spent three hours yesterday with the woman I love, in the presence of a rival whom she wishes me to believe is receiving her favours. There were admittedly bitter moments when I saw her lovely eyes gazing on him, and as I left I felt keen pangs of misery and despair. But what a host of new things! What vivid thoughts, and swift arguments! In spite of my rival's apparent good fortune, I felt with a rush of pride and delight that my love was far greater than his. I told myself that those cheeks would grow pale with fear at even the least of the sacrifices my love would joyfully make. For instance, I would gladly plunge my hand into a hat to take out one of two tickets: '*Be loved by her*' or '*Die at once*', and this feeling is so well established that I was able to make myself agreeable and take part in the conversation.

'If anyone had told me all this two years ago I should have laughed derisively.'

In the account of the voyage made by Captains Lewis and Clarke in 1806 to the sources of the Missouri, I read this on page 215: 'Though poor, the *Ricaras* are kind and generous, and we stayed some time in three of their villages. Their women are the most beautiful of any tribe we have encountered. Moreover they are disinclined to keep their lovers in suspense. We found a further proof of the saying that to see the world is to discover that nothing is immutable. Among the *Ricaras*, it is a great breach of good behaviour for a woman to grant her favours without the consent of her husband or brother. But, on the other hand, the husbands and brothers are delighted to be able to offer this little courtesy to their friends.

'There was a negro in our party who made a great impression on a people who had never seen a man of that colour before. He was soon the favourite of the fair sex, and we observed that, far from displaying jealousy, the husbands were delighted when he visited their homes. The whole situation was enlivened by the fact that in such ramshackle huts as theirs everything was open to view.'

CHAPTER 10
Love at Loggerheads

Where there are quarrels in love these are of two kinds:
1. When the one who starts the quarrel is in love.
2. When the quarreller is not in love.

Where one of the lovers has too much advantage over the other in certain qualities which they both value, the other's love will die because sooner or later fear of contempt will abruptly stop the process of crystallization.

Nothing is more hateful to mediocre people than intellectual superiority in others; it is, in our society, the very fountain-head of hatred. If this principle does not breed atrocious hatreds it is only because the people divided thereby are not obliged to live together. But consider what happens in love where natural behaviour is not masked and where the superior partner, in particular, does not conceal his superiority behind social wariness.

If the passion is to survive, the inferior lover must ill-treat the other, who will otherwise be unable even to close a window without giving offence.

As a superior lover you will create illusions, and not only will your love run no risks, but the very weakness of your beloved will strengthen the bond between you.

For sheer durability, passionate requited love between people of the same calibre takes first place. *Love at loggerheads*, where the quarreller does not love, comes a close second. You will find examples of this in stories about the Duchesse de Berry in the *Memoirs* of Duclos. This kind of love, having as it does something of the coldness of habit which springs from the prosaic and selfish parts of life which follow a man to his grave, may last longer than passionate love itself. In fact it is no longer love but merely a habit caused by love, whose only relation to the original passion is one of memories and physical pleasure. The existence of this habit necessarily presupposes natures of lesser nobility. Every day some little crisis may occur: 'Will he scold me . . . ?' which, as in passionate love, keeps the imagination busy; and every day some new proof of tenderness has to be given. See the anecdotes about Mme d'Houdetot and Saint-Lambert.

Occasionally pride may refuse to stoop to this sort of thing; then, after a few stormy months, pride kills love. But you will find that the nobler passion makes prolonged resistance before it succumbs. A lover who is still in love, despite ill-treatment, will long continue to foster an illusion about 'little tiffs'. A few tender reconciliations can help to make the transition bearable. On the plea of some secret sorrow or stroke of ill-luck, you forgive the person you have loved so much; in the end you become accustomed to a cat-and-dog life. After all, barring passionate love, gambling, and the enjoyment of power, where would you find so rich a source of daily interest? If the aggressor dies, you will notice that the surviving victim is inconsolable. This principle is the successful basis of many middle-class marriages; the scolded ones have to listen all day to their favourite topic.

There is also a kind of love that is pseudo-quarrelsome. I have borrowed my Chapter 33 from the letter of an extremely clever woman:

'Always a little doubt to set at rest – that's what keeps one craving in passionate love. Because the keenest misgivings are always there, its pleasures never become tedious.'

With boorish, ill-bred, or very violent people, this little doubt to be set at rest, this slight anxiety, takes the form of a quarrel.

Unless the beloved possesses that extreme subtlety which results from a careful upbringing, she may find this kind of love more lively, and therefore more enjoyable; and however fastidious she may be she will find it very difficult, when she sees her *furious* lover the first to suffer from his own violent emotions, not to love him the more for it. Perhaps what Lord Mortimer misses most about his mistress are the candlesticks she used to throw at his head. Indeed, if pride will pardon and allow sensations such as these, it must be admitted that they wage a bitter war against boredom, the great affliction of contented people.

Saint-Simon, the only historian France has ever possessed, says: 'After many passing fancies the Duchesse de Berry had fallen deeply in love with Riom, a junior member of the d'Aydie family, the son of one of Madame de Biron's sisters. He had neither looks nor brains; he was fat, short, chubby-cheeked, and pale, and had such a crop of pimples that he seemed one large abscess; he had beautiful teeth, but not the least idea that he was going to inspire a passion which quickly got out of control, a passion which lasted a lifetime, notwithstanding a number of subsidiary flirtations and affairs. He hadn't a penny to bless himself with, and his numerous brothers and sisters were as poor as he. The Duchess's tirewoman and her husband, Mme and M. de Pons, were related to them, and came from the same part of the country. Hoping to make something of the young man, who was then a lieutenant in the dragoons, they invited him to stay with them. No sooner had he arrived than he took the Duchess's fancy and became master in the Luxembourg.

'M. de Lauzun, whose great-nephew he was, laughed up his sleeve about all this. He was overjoyed, and in the young man saw himself all over again, as he used to be at the Luxembourg in the days of the great Mademoiselle. He used to advise the boy what to do, and Riom, who was naturally gentle, polite, and respectful, paid heed to him like the honest lad he was. But very soon he grew aware of the power his charms conferred, with their unique appeal to the unaccountable fancy of the princess. He did not exercise this power unfairly over others and became popular with everyone, though he used to treat his duchess as M. de Lauzun had treated Mademoiselle. He was soon attired in the richest lace and the finest garments, and provided with money, jewellery, and buckles. He would excite but not requite the desire of the princess; he delighted in making her jealous, or pretending to be jealous himself. He would often drive her to tears. Gradually he forced her into the position of doing nothing without his leave, even trifles of no importance. Sometimes, when she was ready to go to the Opéra, he insisted that she stay at home; and sometimes he made her go there against her will. He obliged her to grant favours to ladies she did not like or of whom she was jealous, and to deny favours to people she did like, of whom he pretended to be jealous. She was not even free to dress as she chose; he would amuse himself by making her change her coiffure or her dress at the last minute; he did this so often and so publicly that she became accustomed to take his orders in the evening for what she would do and wear the following day; then the next day he would alter everything, and the princess would cry all the more. In the end she took to sending him messages by trusted footmen, for from the first he had taken up residence in the Luxembourg; messages which continued throughout her toilette, to know what ribbons she would wear, what gown and what other ornaments; almost invariably he made her wear something she did not wish to. When she occasionally dared to do anything, however small, without his leave, he treated her like a servant, and she was in tears for several days.

'This proud princess, whose pleasure was to behave with the greatest arrogance, demeaned herself to attend obscure dinners with him among a crowd of ne'er-do-wells, this woman with whom no one was permitted to sit at table unless he were a prince of the blood.

Riglet, a Jesuit whom she had known as a child and who cultivated her, was invited to these private dinner-parties, without shame or embarrassment on either side. Madame de Mouchy was privy to all the strange goings-on; she and Riom would invite the guests and name the days, and she used to patch up the lovers' quarrels. All this was common knowledge in the Luxembourg, where Riom was sought after by everyone; he in his turn took care to be on good terms with everybody, behaving to all others with a respect which he publicly denied only to his princess. Before the assembled company he would give her such brusque replies that everyone lowered their eyes, and the Duchess would blush, though her passion for him was in no way curtailed.'

For the princess, Riom was a sovereign remedy against boredom.

When Bonaparte was a young hero covered with glory and still innocent of any crime against liberty, a famous woman suddenly blurted out to him: 'General, a woman must be either your wife or your sister!' The hero did not understand the compliment, which brought some fine insults upon his head. Women of this kind love to be despised by their lovers and can only love cruel men.

CHAPTER II
Cures for Love

In ancient times the Leucadian Leap was an apt image. It is, indeed, almost impossible to find a cure for love. Not only must there be danger, to remind a man forcibly of the need for self-preservation, but, and this is much more difficult to find, it must be a continually pressing danger, yet one which a man can skilfully avoid for long enough to re-acquire the habit of thinking about the need for survival. In my opinion nothing less than a sixteen-day storm as in Don Juan, or M. Cochelet's shipwreck among the Moors will suffice; otherwise you very soon become inured to danger, and in the front line, twenty paces from the enemy, you again begin thinking of your beloved even more devotedly than ever.

We have repeated over and over again that when a man really loves he *rejoices* or *trembles* no matter what he thinks about; and everything in Nature speaks to him of his beloved. Now rejoicing and trembling are interesting activities beside which all others pale.

A friend who wishes to cure lovesickness must in the first place always be on the side of the beloved woman, and yet friends with more zeal than shrewdness never fail to do the opposite. This is simply to attack, with ludicrously inadequate forces, that pattern of exquisite illusion which we have previously called crystallization.

The healing friend must always keep in mind that where the lover has a choice between swallowing some absurdity or giving up all that makes life worth living, he will swallow it and use all his intelligence to disprove his mistress's most obvious vices and most blatant infidelities. This is how in passionate love everything is forgiven after a little while.

Men of cold rational temperament will only accept vices in their mistresses after several months of passion.

Far from seeking crudely and openly to distract the lover, the healing friend should rather talk to him *ad nauseam* about both his love and his mistress, and at the same time contrive a whole succession of trivial happenings around him. If travel *isolates* it is no cure, and indeed nothing is more tenderly reminiscent of the beloved than changes of scene. It is in brilliant Paris salons, among the reputedly most charming women, that I have felt the greatest love for my own poor mistress, solitary and sad in her little lodging in the depths of the Romagna.

An exile in a splendid salon, I used to watch the magnificent clock for the exact moment when she would be leaving her lodging on foot, even in the rain, to visit her friend. In seeking to forget her I discovered that changes of scene provided memories, less vivid but far more sublime than those evoked in places where we had once met.

For absence to be of any use, the healing friend must

always be on hand to keep commenting as much as possible on the events which have taken place in the love affair, and to ensure that these reflections are long, wearisome, and pointless, so that they begin to sound like commonplace. Tender sentimentality, for example, could be used after a dinner party enlivened with good wines.

The difficulty of forgetting a woman with whom you have been happy is that the imagination tirelessly continues to evoke and embellish moments of the past.

I shall say nothing about pride, a cruel though certain cure, but not one for sensitive people.

The early scenes of Shakespeare's *Romeo* are an admirable illustration. It is a far cry from the man who tells himself sadly: 'She hath forsworn to love' to the one who exclaims at the pinnacle of his happiness: 'Come what sorrow can!'

CHAPTER 12
Maxims of Love

Under this title, which I wish were more modest still, I have gathered a fairly generous selection from three or four hundred playing-cards scribbled over in pencil. Often what for want of a better name must be called the original manuscript consists of variously-sized pieces of paper written in pencil, which Lisio stuck together with wax to save himself the trouble of transcribing. He once told me that nothing he jotted down seemed an hour later to have been worth the effort of transcription. I mention this detail in the hope that it will serve to excuse the repetitions.

I

Everything can be acquired in solitude, except character.

2

In 1821; hatred, love, and avarice, the three most common passions; together with gambling, almost the only ones in Rome.

At first sight the Romans seem *wicked*; but in fact they are only mistrustful in the extreme, with an imagination that flares up on the slightest pretext.

If one of them is *wantonly* wicked it is because he is frightened and is trying to reassure himself by testing his gun.

3

If I were to say, as I believe, that kindliness is the distinguishing characteristic of Parisians, I am afraid I should offend them.

'I don't want to be kind!'

4

A sign of love has just struck me; it is when all the pleasures and all the pains attributable to all the other passions and all the other needs of a man cease abruptly to affect him.

5

Prudishness is a kind of avarice – the worst kind.

6

A dependable character is one which has a long and unshakable experience of life's disappointments and misfortunes. Such a man desires constantly or not at all.

7

Love as it exists in high society is a love of duelling or a love of gambling.

8

Nothing is more fatal to mannered love than gusts of passionate love in the partner.

Contessina L. Forli, 1819

9

A serious failing in women, the most shocking of all for a man worthy of the name. In matters of feeling, the public seldom rises above the level of meanness in ideas; yet women appoint the public as supreme judge of their lives. This applies even to the most distinguished women who are often quite unaware of it, and even believe and declare that the contrary is true.

Brescia, 1819

10

Prosaic is a new word which I used to think ridiculous, since there is nothing colder than our poetry; if there has been any warmth in France during the last fifty years it is certainly in our prose.

But the contessina Léonore used the word *prosaic*, and I love to write it.

The definition of it is in *Don Quixote* and in the '*Perfect contrast between master and squire.*' The master, tall and pale; the squire, fat and ruddy. The former all heroism and courtliness; the latter all selfishness and servility; the first brimming with moving and romantic dreams; the second a model of good behaviour, a very symposium of prudent proverbs; the one for ever fortifying his spirit with some heroic and perilous contemplation; the other mulling over some careful course of action in which he does not fail to allow meticulously for the influence of every little shameful and selfish motive known to the human heart.

When the former ought to be disabused by the *non-success* of his dreams of yesterday, he is already fully occupied with today's castles in Spain.

It is better to have a prosaic husband and to take a romantic lover.

Marlborough had a *prosaic* mind; Henri IV, in love at fifty-five with a young princess well aware of his age, had a romantic heart.

There are fewer prosaic minds among the nobility than among the middle class.

That is the disadvantage of trade; it makes one prosaic.

II

Nothing is so interesting as passion; everything about it is so unexpected, and its agent is also its victim. Nothing could be duller than mannered love, where everything is calculated, as in all the prosaic affairs of everyday life.

12

By the end of a visit one always finishes by treating one's suitor better than was intended.

L. 2nd November 1818

13

The influence of his class is always apparent in a parvenu, despite any genius he may have. Look at the way Rousseau fell in love with all the 'ladies' he met, or at his tears of joy because the Duke of Luxembourg, one of the dullest courtiers of the day, condescended to walk on the right instead of on the left, with a M. Coindet, a friend of Rousseau's.

L. 3rd May 1820

14

Ravenna, 23rd January 1820

Women here have no education except in material things; a mother has no scruples about showing despair or ecstatic joy, for love's sake, before her twelve- to fifteen-year-old daughters. Remember that in this happy clime many women are still very attractive at forty-five, and that most of them are married by the age of eighteen.

La Valchiusa, talking yesterday of Lampugnani: 'Ah, there was the man for me! He really knew how to love ... etc., etc.,' and carrying on this conversation for some time with a friend, in the presence of her daughter, a wide-awake young person of fourteen or fifteen, whom she also used to take along on her sentimental walks with this lover.

Now and then the girls pick up excellent maxims of behaviour. For instance, Madame Guarnacci, with her two daughters and two men whom she never set eyes on before or since, holding forth with profound maxims for half an hour, supported by examples they knew of (that of la Cercara in Hungary), concerning the precise moment when it is most suitable to punish by infidelity a lover who has misbehaved himself.

15

The sanguine type, the true Frenchman (Colonel Mathis), instead of torturing himself with excess of feeling, like Rousseau, when he has an assignation for the following evening at seven, sees everything in a rosy light until the lucky moment. Such people have but little propensity for passionate love; it would disturb their delightful tranquillity. I would go so far as to say they might regard its transports as unhappiness, and certainly they would be humiliated by its shyness.

16

Most men of the world, from vanity, from mistrust, from fear of disillusionment, refrain from falling in love with a woman until after intimacy.

17

The very sensitive need a woman to be easy of access if crystallization is to be encouraged.

18

A woman thinks to recognize the voice of the public in the first fool or false friend who claims to be a faithful interpreter of public opinion.

19

There is delicious pleasure in clasping in your arms a woman who has caused you much suffering, who has been your cruel enemy for a long time, and who is still ready to be so. Happiness of French officers in Spain, 1812.

20

To rejoice in one's heart and to love, one needs solitude, but to be a success one must get about in society.

21

All that the French have written about love has been well written, precise, and without exaggeration; but it has dealt only with superficial affections, said the good Cardinal Lante.

22

The whole *development of passion* in Goldoni's comedy of the *Innamorati* is excellent; it is the style and the thoughts which are so disgustingly and revoltingly mean; it is the opposite of a French comedy.

23

Youth in 1822. A serious inclination, an active disposition, mean a sacrifice of the present to the future; nothing is so elevating for the soul as the power and the habit of making such sacrifices. I see more likelihood of grand passions in 1832 than in 1772.

24

The bilious temperament, when it does not take too repulsive a form, is perhaps the most likely of all to strike and nourish imagination in women. When the bilious temperament does not occur in propitious circumstances like those of Lauzun in Saint-Simon's *Mémoires* (Vol. v, 380) it is difficult to grow accustomed to it. But once this character has been grasped by a woman it is bound to fascinate her: yes, even the wild and fanatical Balfour (*Old Mortality*). For women it is the exact opposite of the prosaic.

25

In love we are often in doubt of what we believe in most strongly (La R. 355). In every other passion, what we have once proved we no longer doubt.

26

Verse was invented as an aid to memory. Later it was preserved to increase pleasure by the spectacle of difficulty overcome. That it should still survive in dramatic art is a vestige of barbarism. Example – the cavalry orders written in verse by M. de Bonnay.

27

While that jealous suitor is regaling himself with boredom, avarice, hatred, and cold, poisonous passions, I spend a happy night dreaming of her – her who ill-treats me because she does not trust me.

– S.

28

Only a great mind dares express itself simply; this is why Rousseau filled *La Nouvelle Héloïse* with so much rhetoric, and this made it unreadable for anyone over thirty.

29

'Certainly the most serious reproach we can level against ourselves is that we should allow ideas of honour and justice, which occasionally well up in our hearts, to vanish like the slightest phantoms of a dream.'

Letter from Jena, March 1819

30

A respectable woman is at her country house and spends an hour in the hot-house with her gardener; people with whom she has been at variance accuse her of having taken the gardener as a lover.

What can she reply? Absolutely speaking, the thing is possible. She might say 'My character is my defence; examine my whole life,' but these things are equally beyond the perception of the wicked who refuse to see and of the fools who cannot see.

Salviati, Rome, 23 *July* 1819

31

I have seen a man discover that his rival was beloved, and the latter fail to perceive it because of his passion.

32

The more desperately a man is in love the greater the violence he must do his own feelings in daring to risk offending the woman he loves by taking her hand.

33

Ludicrous rhetoric but, unlike that of Rousseau, inspired by genuine passion: *Memoirs* of M. de Maubreuil, Sand's letter.

34

Naturalness

This evening I saw, or thought I saw, the triumph of naturalness in a young woman who I must admit seems to be a person of great character. It seems clear to me that she adores a cousin of hers, and she herself must certainly be aware of it. The cousin is in love with her too, but because she behaves towards him with great seriousness he thinks he does not please her and allows himself to be distracted by the advances of one Clara, a young widow who is a friend of Mélanie's. I believe he may marry her; Mélanie sees this and suffers all that a heart can suffer when it is proud and filled with a violent and irresistible passion. She need only change her manner a little, but she considers that to depart even for a moment from *naturalness* would be so contemptible as to demean her for the rest of her life.

35

Sappho saw in love only delirium of the senses or physical pleasure rendered sublime by crystallization. Anacreon regarded it as a recreation for the senses and the intellect. There was too little security in those ancient days to allow a man the leisure for indulging in a passionate love affair.

36

I only need to consider the previous fact to laugh a little at people who think Homer greater than Tasso. Passionate love did exist in Homer's day, and not very far from Greece.

37

Woman of sensibility, you who seek to know whether you are loved passionately by the man you adore, examine your lover's early youth. Every man of distinction was at the beginning of his life either absurdly fanatical or else dogged by misfortune. A man of cheerful, gentle disposition, easy to please, can never love with the passion your heart demands.

I call passion only what has stood the test of protracted misfortunes of a kind carefully avoided by novels, and which indeed novels *cannot* convey.

38

A stern resolve at once changes the direst misfortune into something bearable. On the evening after a lost battle a man is in headlong flight on a spent horse; he can clearly hear a group of horsemen galloping after him; suddenly he stops, dismounts, reloads his carbine and pistols, and resolves to defend himself. His vision of death is instantly changed into that of the cross of the Legion of Honour.

39

Basis of the English way of life. About 1730, when Voltaire and Fontenelle were already with us, a machine was invented in England to separate newly-threshed corn from the chaff; it was worked by a wheel which created enough draught to blow the chaff away; but in that *bible-ridden* country the peasants claimed that it was blasphemous to go against the will of Divine Providence and produce an artificial wind in this way, instead of praying fervently to Heaven for a wind to winnow the corn, and waiting for the moment ordained by the God of Israel. Compare this with the French peasantry.

40

There is no doubt that it is madness for a man to lay himself open to passionate love. Sometimes, however, the cure acts too drastically. Young American girls in the United States are so imbued and fortified with rational ideas that love, the flower of life, has deserted their youth. In Boston a girl can quite safely be left alone with a handsome stranger, in the certainty that she will think of nothing but the income of her future husband.

41

In France men who have lost their wives are sad, while widows on the contrary are gay and happy. Women have a proverb about the felicity of widowhood. There is therefore no equality in the contract of marriage.

42

People who are happy in love have a look of profound concentration, which in a Frenchman means profound sadness.

Dresden, 1818

43

The more one pleases generally, the less one pleases profoundly.

44

The imitativeness of our early years makes us acquire the passions of our parents, even when these passions poison our lives. (Léonore's pride.)

45

The source of *feminine pride* most worthy of respect is the fear of demeaning oneself in a lover's eyes by some hasty step or by some action which he might consider unfeminine.

46

True love makes the thought of death frequent, easy, without terrors; it becomes merely a standard of comparison, the price one would pay for many things.

47

How often have I not exclaimed in a courageous moment: 'If someone were to shoot me through the head with a pistol I should thank him ere I died, if I had time!' Only by loving her less can one be courageous concerning one's beloved.

– S. *February* 1820

48

'I could never fall in love,' a young woman told me; 'Mirabeau and his letters to Sophie have quite put me off great souls.' Those fatal letters struck me with all the force of a personal experience. Look for what you never find in novels: that two years' constancy before intimacy proves you can rely on your lover's heart.

49

Ridicule frightens love away. Ridicule out of the question in Italy; what is good form in Venice is odd at Naples, hence nothing is odd. Consequently nothing which gives pleasure is culpable. It is this which disposes of foolish honour, and of one half of comedy.

50

Children get their way by tears, and when they cannot attract attention they hurt themselves purposely. Young women *pique* themselves with amour-propre.

51

It is often remarked, but for this reason easily forgotten, that sensitive people are daily becoming rarer, and cultured minds more commonplace.

52

Feminine Pride

Bologna, 18th April, two o'clock in the morning
I have just witnessed a striking example but, all things considered, it would take fifteen pages to give a fair account of it. I should prefer, if I had the courage, to record the consequences of what I observed beyond any possibility of doubt. Here then is a conviction which I shall have to give up any thought of communicating. There are too many circumstantial details. This kind of pride is the opposite of French vanity. As far as I can remember, the only work where I have seen it described is the *Mémoires* of Madame Roland, in that part where she relates the little arguments she used to propound as a girl.

53

In France most women think nothing of a young man until they have turned him into a conceited fool. Only then can he flatter their vanity.

– Duclos

54

Modena, 1820

Zilietti told me at midnight, at the house of the charming Marchesina R—: 'I shan't dine with you tomorrow at San-Michele (an inn); yesterday I was joking and talking amusingly to Cl***, and it might make me conspicuous.'

Do not jump to the conclusion that Zilietti is foolish or shy. He is a prudent and wealthy citizen of this happy country.

55

What deserves admiration in America is the form of government and not the society. Elsewhere it is the government that does the harm. They have reversed the parts in Boston, and the government plays the hypocrite in order not to shock society.

56

The young women of Italy, when they fall in love, are entirely subject to natural feelings. At best they can rely for guidance only upon a few excellent maxims picked up by listening at doors.

As though fate had decided that everything here

should combine to preserve *natural* behaviour, they do not read novels because there are none. In Geneva and France, on the contrary, girls fall in love at sixteen in order to make a novel out of life, and at each step, almost at each tear, they ask themselves: 'Am I not just like Julie d'Etanges?'

57

The husband of a young woman who is adored by a lover whom she ill-treats, and whom she will barely allow to kiss her hand, will at best enjoy only the coarsest physical pleasure where the lover would experience the most delicious and ecstatic happiness that exists on earth.

58

The laws of *imagination* are still so little understood that I venture the following observation, which may perhaps be quite wrong.

There seem to be two kinds of imagination:

1. Keen, impetuous, spontaneous imagination, leading instantly to action, chafing and languishing at a delay of even twenty-four hours; rather like Fabio's. It is characterized by impatience, and flares into anger against what it cannot obtain. It perceives external objects but these merely add fuel to its fire; it assimilates them and at once converts them to increase the passion.

2. Imagination which kindles only slowly, but which after a time no longer perceives external objects and succeeds in becoming exclusively concerned with, and

dependent on, its own passion. This kind of imagination is quite compatible with slowness and even scarcity of ideas. It is conducive to constancy. It is to be found in most of those poor young German girls who die of love and consumption. This dismal spectacle, so frequent beyond the Rhine, is never seen in Italy.

59

Habits of imagination. A Frenchman is *genuinely* shocked by eight changes of scenery in one act of a tragedy. He finds it impossible to enjoy seeing *Macbeth*, and consoles himself by *damning* Shakespeare.

60

The provinces in France are forty years behind Paris in everything relating to women. A married woman in Corbeil told me that she had only allowed herself to read certain passages of Lauzun's *Mémoires*. Such stupidity stunned and bereft me of all reply; it's really not a book one can put down at will like that.

Failure to act naturally, great fault of provincial women. Their profusion of airs and graces. The leading lights in any town worse than the rest.

61

Goethe, or any other German genius, values money at its true worth. One must think of nothing but making money until one has an income of six thousand francs a year, and after that think of it no further. The fool, for his part, does not understand the advantage of feeling and thinking like Goethe; all his life he thinks and feels only in terms of money. It is by this process of double franchise that the prosaic in society seem to carry the day against those of noble heart.

62

In Europe desire is whetted by constraint; in America it is blunted by liberty.

63

The young have become possessed by a kind of mania for debate which distracts them from love. While they are considering whether Napoleon was useful to France, they let the age for loving slip by; even among those who are disposed to be young the affectations of cravat, spur, and martial aspect, the preoccupation with self, all make them forget to glance at a girl walking demurely by, taking the weekly outing which is all her slender fortunes will permit.

64

I have withheld the chapter entitled *Prude*, and several others.

I am glad to have found the following passage in the memoirs of Horace Walpole:

The two Elizabeths. Let us compare the daughters of two ferocious men, and see which was sovereign of a civilized nation, which of a barbarous one. Both were Elizabeths. The daughter of Peter (of Russia) was absolute yet spared a competitor and a rival; and thought the person of an empress had sufficient allurements for as many of her subjects as she chose to honour with the communication. Elizabeth of England could neither forgive the claim of Mary Stuart nor her charms, but ungenerously emprisoned her (as George IV did Napoleon), when imploring protection and, without the sanction of either despotism or law, sacrificed many to her great and little jealousy. Yet this Elizabeth piqued herself on chastity; and while she practised every ridiculous art of coquetry to be admired at an unseemly age, kept off lovers whom she encouraged, and neither gratified her own desires nor their ambition. Who can help preferring the honest, open-hearted barbarian empress?

(Lord Oxford's *Memoirs*)

65

Excessive familiarity can destroy *crystallization*. A charming girl of sixteen was becoming too fond of a handsome young man of the same age, who used to make a practice of passing beneath her window every evening at nightfall. Her mother invited him to spend a week with them in the country. It was a bold remedy, I admit, but the girl was of a romantic disposition, and the young man a trifle dull; within three days she despised him.

66

Bologna, 17th April 1817

Ave Maria (TWILIGHT), in Italy the hour for tenderness, for the pleasures of the soul and for melancholy: sensation enhanced by the sound of those lovely bells.

Hours for pleasures unrelated to the senses except through memories.

67

The first love affair of a young man entering society is generally one of ambition. It is seldom directed towards a gentle, lovable, innocent girl. How can one tremble, adore, and be aware of oneself in the presence of a divinity? An adolescent needs to love someone whose qualities raise him in his own estimation. It is in a man's declining years that he returns sadly to a love of the simple and the innocent, despairing of the sublime. Between the two comes true love, which thinks of nothing but itself.

68

Greatness of soul is never apparent, for it conceals itself; a little originality is usually all that shows. Greatness of soul is more frequent than one would suppose.

69

Oh, that moment when first you press the hand of the woman you love! The only comparable happiness is that exquisite enjoyment of power which ministers and monarchs affect to despise. This happiness also has its *crystallization* process, requiring a colder and more rational imagination. Think of a man whom, a quarter of an hour earlier, Napoleon has appointed to ministerial office.

70

Nature has given strength to the North and wit to the South, the celebrated Jean de Muller said to me at Cassel in 1808.

71

Nothing could be more fallacious than the saying 'no man is a hero to his valet,' or rather nothing could be more true in *monarchical* terms: the affected hero, like Hippolyte in *Phèdre*. Desaix, for example, would have been a hero even to his valet (admittedly I do not know whether he had one), and indeed more of a hero to his valet than to anyone else. But for good form and the necessary degree of comedy, Turenne and Fénelon might each have been Desaix.

72

Here is a piece of blasphemy: I, a Dutchman, make bold to say that the French take no real pleasure either in conversation or in the theatre; instead of recreation and perfect relaxation it is hard labour. Among the burdens which hastened the death of Madame de Staël, I have heard counted the strain of making conversation during her last winter.

W.

73

The degree of tension necessary in the nerves of the ear to listen to each note, adequately explains the physical aspect of the enjoyment of music.

74

What degrades women of easy virtue is their own conviction, and that of others, that they are committing a great sin.

75

In the army, during a retreat, if you warn an Italian soldier of a danger which it is futile to risk, he will almost thank you, and carefully avoid it. If out of common humanity you point out the same danger to a French soldier he will think you are challenging him, his self-esteem will be *piqued*, and he will immediately expose himself to the danger in question. If he dared he would jeer at you.

Gyat, 1812

76

Any really useful idea, if it can be expressed only in very simple terms, will certainly be despised in France. *Mutual Instruction* would never have caught on had it been discovered by a Frenchman. It is exactly the opposite in Italy.

77

However little passion you may feel for a woman, provided your imagination has not run dry, if she be inept enough to say to you one evening, tenderly and bashfully: 'All right; come tomorrow at noon. I shall be alone,' you will be unable to sleep, and quite incapable of thought. After a morning of torment the hour strikes, and it is as if each stroke were reverberating through your diaphragm.

78

Between lovers the *sharing* of money increases love; the *giving* of money *destroys* love.

In one case present misfortune and, for the future, the grim prospect of the fear of want are dismissed; in the other case an element of *politics* is introduced, an awareness of being two which negates fellow-feeling.

79

(*Messe des Tuileries*, 1811)

The court functions at which women display their bare bosoms very much as officers do their uniforms – and, despite all their charms, with very little more effect – inevitably recall scenes from Aretino.

This is what people will do to curry a man's favour *for mercenary ends*; here is a whole society acting without morality and above all without passion. All this, added to the presence of women in low-cut dresses and bearing the stamp of viciousness, women who greet with a sardonic laugh everything but self-interest promptly paid with material pleasures, reminds one of scenes in the Bagnio, and drives far away any difficulty arising from virtue or the inner satisfaction of a mind at peace with itself.

I have noticed that a feeling of isolation in the midst of all this predisposes sensitive hearts to love.

80

If the soul is engaged in feeling false shame and in overcoming it, it cannot experience pleasure. Pleasure is a luxury; it requires for its enjoyment that security, which is a necessity, should not be imperilled.

81

A sign of love which self-interested women do not know how to simulate. Does reconciliation bring true joy? Or is there a weighing of the advantages to be gained from it?

82

The poor unfortunates who inhabit the monastery of La Trappe are wretched people who have not had quite enough courage to kill themselves. I except the leaders, who enjoy the pleasure of being leaders.

83

To have known Italian beauty is a misfortune; one becomes insensitive. Except in Italy one prefers the conversation of men.

84

Italian prudence tends towards self-preservation, which allows the imagination free play. (See an account of the death of the famous comic actor Pertica, 24th December 1821.) English prudence on the other hand, entirely concerned to amass and conserve enough money to cover expenses, demands a meticulous and unremitting precision, a habit which paralyses the imagination. But note that at the same time it lends the greatest strength to the idea of *duty*.

85

Immense respect for money, which is the besetting sin of the English and the Italians, is less noticeable in France, and entirely diminished to its just importance in Germany.

86

Frenchwomen, never having known the happiness of *genuine* passion, are not exacting about the happiness of their own households, nor about *everyday* life.

Compiègne

87

'You may well talk of ambition as an antidote to boredom,' said Kamensky; 'I used to gallop two leagues every evening to visit the princess at Kolich, and all the time I was in the intimate society of a despot whom I respected and in whose hands lay all my happiness and the power to satisfy my every possible desire.'

Wilna, 1812

88

Perfection in their attention to minor manners and dress, great kindness, no great intelligence, attentiveness to a hundred little details every day, inability to be interested for more than three days in any one event; a pretty contrast with puritan severity, biblical cruelty, strict probity, shy and painful self-consciousness, universal *cant*; and yet these are the two greatest peoples in the world!

89

Since among princesses there has been a Catherine the Second who was an empress, why should there not have been among the bourgeoises a female Samuel Bernard or Lagrange?

90

Alviza calls it an unforgivable lack of delicacy to dare write letters in which you speak of love to a woman whom you adore, and who swears, gazing at you tenderly the while, that she will never love you.

91

The greatest philosopher the French have ever had unfortunately did not live in some distant Alpine solitude, nor launch his book from there upon Paris without ever entering the city himself. When they saw Helvétius so simple and honest, affected and precious people like Suard, Marmontel and Diderot could never believe that here was a great philosopher. In all sincerity they doubted the profundity of his thought; in the first place it was simple, an unforgivable sin in France; in the second place the man – and not his book – was subject to one weakness: he attached excessive importance to what is known in France as glory, to being fashionable among his contemporaries such as Balzac, Voiture and Fontenelle.

Rousseau had too much sensibility and too little common-sense, Buffon was too hypocritical about his botanical garden, Voltaire too childish, for any of them to be capable of judging Helvétius's principle.

This philosopher made the little mistake of calling his principle *self-interest* instead of giving it the prettier name of *pleasure*, but what can we think of the common-sense of a whole literary culture which allows itself to be misled by such a little slip of the pen?

A man of ordinary intelligence, Prince Eugene of Savoy for example, if he were in Regulus's shoes, would have stayed quietly in Rome, where he might even have derided the folly of the senate in Carthage; but Regulus went back. Prince Eugene would have been pursuing his own *interest* exactly as Regulus pursued his.

In nearly every situation in life a generous person will perceive a possible course of action of which the ordinary man has not the least inkling. The instant this course of action becomes clear to the generous person it is in *his interest* to take it.

If he did not perform the action once he had perceived it, he would despise himself and be unhappy. One's duties are in direct proportion to the scope of one's intelligence. The principle of Helvétius holds good even in the most frenzied ecstasies of love, even in the case of suicide. It is against his nature, it is impossible that man should not always, at any given moment, do what in that moment is possible and which gives him the most pleasure.

92

To have a strong character one must have experienced the effect produced by others upon oneself; therefore others are a necessity.

93

Love in Ancient Times

The love letters of Roman matrons have never been posthumously published. Petronius wrote a charming book, but has depicted only debauchery.

As regards *love* in Rome, apart from Dido and the second Eclogue of Virgil, we have nothing more precise to go on than the writings of the three great poets Ovid, Tibullus, and Propertius.

Now the elegies of Parny or the letter from Héloïse to Abelard by Colardeau are very incomplete and vague descriptions by comparison with certain letters from *La Nouvelle Héloïse* or those of a Portuguese nun, Mlle de Lespinasse, Mirabeau's Sophie, Werther, etc.

Poetry, with its compulsory similes, its mythology in which the poet does not believe, its dignified Louis XIV style, and its whole paraphernalia of so-called poetic embellishment, is far less effective than prose in giving a clear and precise idea of the emotions of the heart; and in this sphere only clarity can move one.

Tibullus, Ovid, and Propertius had better taste than our poets; they showed love as it could have existed among the proud citizens of Rome; yet they lived under Augustus who, having closed the temple of Janus, sought to resorb the citizens into a state of loyal subjection to a monarchy.

The mistresses of these three great poets were unfaithful, venal coquettes from whom the poets sought only physical pleasure, and I am inclined to believe that they never had an inkling of the sublime feelings which throbbed thirteen centuries later in the heart of tender Héloïse.

The following passage is borrowed from a distinguished man of letters who knows the Latin poets far better than I:

'The brilliant genius of Ovid, the rich imagination of Propertius and the sensitive soul of Tibullus undoubtedly led them to write verse subtly different from each other's, but each loved a woman of almost the same type in the same way. They desired, they triumphed, they had fortunate rivals, they were jealous, they quarrelled and were reconciled, they were unfaithful in their turn, were forgiven and regained a contentment that was soon disturbed by the recurrence of the same happenings.

'Corinna is married. The first lesson Ovid teaches her is how she must cunningly deceive her husband; what signs they must employ in his presence and in public so that they may understand each other and yet be understood only by each other. Fulfilment follows soon after, then quarrels; then something unexpected from so gallant a man as Ovid, insults and blows; then apologies, tears and forgiveness. Sometimes he calls upon servants and underlings: his mistress's doorkeeper, to let him in at night; an accursed old woman who corrupts her and teaches her to sell herself for gold; an old eunuch who guards her; a young slave-girl, to deliver writing-tablets requesting a meeting. The request is refused and he curses the tablets which have met with so little success. Later he is more fortunate, and exhorts Dawn not to interrupt his happiness.

'Soon he begins to accuse himself of frequent infidelities and of having a taste for all women. A moment later Corinna is also unfaithful; he cannot bear the thought of having taught her lessons from which she is now profiting in another's arms. Corinna in her turn is jealous; she behaves more like an angry woman than a tender one and accuses him of being in love with a young slave-girl. He swears that he is nothing of the sort, and writes to the slave-girl; and all that had angered Corinna turns out to be true after all. How can she have found out? What signs betrayed them? He insists that the slave-girl shall grant him a further meeting, and threatens, if she will not, to confess everything to Corinna. He jokes with a friend about his two loves and the hardships and pleasures they bring him. Shortly afterwards he is solely engrossed with Corinna. She is all his. He sings his triumph as though it were his first victory. After certain happenings which for several reasons are best left in Ovid's text, and others which it would take too long to relate, he finds that Corinna's husband has become too acquiescent, and is no longer jealous. This displeases the lover who threatens to leave the man's wife unless he renews his jealousy. The husband obeys him to excess and has Corinna so closely watched that Ovid can no longer

get near her. He complains of the surveillance he himself has provoked, but is sure he can outwit it; unfortunately he is not the only one to succeed in doing so.
Corinna's infidelities begin again, more frequent than
before, and her affairs become so public that Ovid begs
her at least to grant him the favour of trying a little
harder to deceive him, and of making it a little less
obvious what she really is. This was the way of life of
Ovid and his mistress, and such was the character of
their loves.

'Cynthia is the first love of Propertius, and is to be
the last. As soon as he is granted happiness he begins
to be jealous. Cynthia is too fond of fine clothes; he
begs her to eschew luxury and to love simplicity. He
himself is given to more than one kind of debauchery.
Cynthia is waiting for him but he does not arrive until
morning, straight from the table and far gone in wine.
He finds her asleep, and it is some time before she is
awoken by all the noise he makes or even by the caresses
he gives her. At last she opens her eyes and reproaches
him as he deserves. A friend tries to estrange him from
Cynthia; he waxes eloquent to this friend about her
beauty and her talents. He is faced with the threat of
losing her when she elopes with a soldier; she becomes
a camp-follower and exposes herself to every indignity
in the pursuit of her soldier. Propertius is not angry,
but weeps and makes vows so that she shall be happy.
He swears he will not leave the house from which she
has departed; he will seek out strangers who have seen
her, and ply them with questions about Cynthia. Her
heart is touched by so great a love; she leaves the soldier

and remains with the poet. Intoxicated with happiness he thanks Apollo and the Muses. This happiness is soon disturbed by new crises of jealousy, culminating in estrangement and parting. Absent from her he can think of nothing but Cynthia. Her past infidelities lead him to fear that she will commit new ones. Death holds no fears for him and his only anxiety is lest he lose Cynthia; if he could be sure she would be faithful to him he would gladly go to his grave.

'After further betrayals he thinks he is released from his love, but very soon resumes his shackles, painting the most ravishing portrait of his mistress, with her beauty, her elegant dress, her talent for singing, poetry, and dancing, each redoubling and vindicating his love. But Cynthia, as perverse as she is attractive, disgraces herself in the eyes of the whole city by such scandalous adventures that Propertius can no longer love her without shame. He blushes for it, but he cannot tear himself away from her. He will be her lover – her husband – never will he love anyone but Cynthia. They leave each other, and come together again. Cynthia is jealous, and he reassures her: he will never love another woman. It is indeed no single woman that he loves, but *all* women. He can never possess enough of them, and his need for pleasures is insatiable. He is only brought to himself when Cynthia again throws him over, and then his protests are as loud as if he had never been unfaithful himself. He wants to escape and seeks distraction in debauchery, having as usual drunk too much. He pretends that he is met by a host of Cupids who bring him back to Cynthia's feet. Their reconciliation is followed by renewed storms. While they are supping together Cynthia, as overheated with wine as he is himself, upsets the table and throws goblets at his head, which he finds charming. In the end further treacheries oblige him to break his bond; he must get away, and decides to make a journey to Greece; but when all his plans are complete he gives up the idea, only to find himself the victim of new injuries. Cynthia no longer confines herself to betraying him, but makes him a laughing-stock in the eyes of his rivals, until she is stricken with an illness and dies. She reproaches him for his infidelities and his capriciousness, for having abandoned her in her last hours, and swears that she herself, despite all appearances, was always faithful to him. Such are the adventures and behaviour of Propertius and his mistress, and such is the abridged account of their loves. So much for the woman whom a being of Propertius' calibre was reduced to loving.

'Ovid and Propertius were often unfaithful, but never inconstant. They were two confirmed libertines who often bestowed their favours at random, but who always returned to resume the same shackles. Corinna and Cynthia had to withstand the rivalry of all women, but not of any one woman in particular. The Muse of these two poets was faithful, even if their love was not, and no other name than that of Corinna or Cynthia appears in their verse. Tibullus, a more sensitive lover and poet, less lively and less wanton in his tastes, cannot boast the same constancy. One after another three beauties become the focus of his love and of his verse. The first and most famous is Delia, who is also the best loved. Tibullus has lost his fortune, but he still has the countryside and Delia; his only wishes are that he may possess her in the peace of the fields, that he may press her hand in his as he dies, and that she may follow his funeral procession in tears. Delia is placed in confinement by a jealous husband; he resolves to break into her prison despite the watchdogs and the triple locks, and in her arms to forget all his cares. He falls ill, and Delia alone preoccupies his thoughts. He urges her to remain chaste, *to despise gold*, to grant to him alone what he has obtained from her. But Delia does not take this advice. He had thought he could bear her unfaithfulness, but is overwhelmed and begs Delia and Venus to have mercy on him. In vain he seeks solace in wine; he can neither soften his regrets nor cure his love. He seeks out Delia's husband, who has been deceived like himself, and explains all the tricks she uses to attract and entertain her lovers. If the husband cannot keep her let him hand her over to Tibullus' care; the latter will know how to put the lovers off and keep safe from their snares the woman who has outraged them both. He grows calmer, and more reconciled to her; and remembers Delia's mother who used to champion their love; the recollection of this good woman re-opens his heart to tenderness and all Delia's ill-doings are forgotten. But she is soon guilty of further and graver transgressions. She has allowed herself to be corrupted by gold and presents; she gives herself to another, then to others. Tibullus finally breaks a shameful bondage and bids her farewell for ever.

'He falls under the spell of Nemesis and is none the happier; gold is her only love and she cares little for verses and the gifts of genius. Nemesis is a miserly woman who sells herself to the highest bidder; though he curses her avarice he loves her, and cannot live unless she will love him in return. He resolves to move her with touching pictures. She has lost her young sister, and he will go and weep over her grave, confiding his woes to the mute ashes. Her sister's shade will be displeased by the tears shed on Nemesis' account, and Nemesis should not regard that displeasure lightly, for the mournful ghost of her sister would visit her at night and disturb her sleep . . . But these sad memories wring tears from Nemesis, and he cannot bring himself to buy even happiness at such a price. His third mistress is Neaera. For a long time he basks in his love for her, and asks nothing more from the gods than that he may live and die with her, but she leaves him and goes away. He can think of no one else, and her name fills his prayers; he dreams that Apollo comes to tell him that Neaera has left him for ever, but he refuses to believe the dream, for he could never survive such a catastrophe; and yet the catastrophe has happened. Neaera is unfaithful, and he has once again been deserted. Such were the character of Tibullus and his fate, and such the triple and somewhat dismal story of his loves.

'It is chiefly Tibullus who is dominated by gentle melancholy, which lends even his pleasure that tinge of reverie and sadness wherein lies the charm. If any poet of antiquity can be said to have introduced morality into love, that poet was Tibullus; but those nuances of feeling which he expresses so well are *in himself*, and he is no more concerned than the other two to find or induce such nuances in his mistresses. Their graces and their beauty are what inflames him; their favours are what he covets or regrets; their faithlessness, venality, and wantonness are what tortures him. Of all these women immortalized in the verse of three great poets, Cynthia appears to be the most attractive. In addition to her other charms she has that of her talents; she cultivates singing and poetry; but for all these talents, which were fairly common among courtesans of a certain class, she is no more worthy; pleasure, gold, and wine are none the less her ruling passions; and Propertius, who only once or twice boasts of this taste she has for the arts, is none the less, in his passion for her, enslaved by quite another kind of power.'

These great poets were apparently among the most sensitive and fastidious souls of their time, and yet these were the women they loved and this was how they loved. All literary considerations must here be set aside. I am only looking to them for testimony about their times; two thousand years hence a novel by Ducray-Duminil will be testimony about our customs.

93a

One of my great regrets is not to have been able to see Venice in 1760, a sequence of lucky accidents had apparently combined within that tiny area both the political institutions and the opinions most favourable to man's happiness. A gentle voluptuousness brought happiness within easy reach of all. There was no internal conflict and no crime. Every brow was serene, no one was anxious to appear wealthier, and hypocrisy was pointless. I imagine that it must have been exactly the opposite of London in 1822.

94

If for a lack of personal security you substitute a healthy fear of lacking money, you will see that the United States of America, as regards the passion which is the subject of our present monograph, bears a strong resemblance to the ancient world.

In speaking of the more or less imperfect sketches of passionate love left to us by the ancients I see that I have omitted to mention the *Loves of Medea* in the *Golden Fleece*. Virgil copied them for his Dido. Compare this with love as it appears in a modern novel. *Le Doyen de Killerine*, for example.

95

The Roman feels the beauty of Nature and the arts with surprising strength, depth, and accuracy, but if he sets about trying rationally to discuss what he feels so forcefully the result is pitiful.

Perhaps it is because his feelings come from Nature, and his logic from the government.

One sees at once why the fine arts, outside Italy, are nothing but a bad joke; they are more rationally discussed, but the public cannot *feel*.

96

London, 20th November 1821

A very sensible man who has just arrived from Madras told me yesterday in two hours what I summarize below in twenty lines or so:

That *dreariness* which weighs inexplicably upon the character of the English is so deeply ingrained in their hearts that even in Madras, at the other end of the world, when an Englishman can obtain a few days' furlough he hastens to leave the rich and thriving city of Madras and to find relaxation in the little French town of Pondicherry which flourishes, without natural resources and almost without commerce, under the paternal administration of M. Dupuy. In Madras they drink Burgundy at thirty-six francs a bottle, while the poverty of the French in Pondicherry is such that even in the best circles the refreshments consist mostly of large glasses of water. But there is laughter there.

Nowadays there is more liberty in England than in Prussia. The climate is the same as that of Köenigsberg, Berlin, and Warsaw, none of which is noted for its cheerlessness. The working classes in these cities have less security and drink just as little wine as in England, and they are much less well-clothed.

Aristocratic circles in Venice and Vienna are not sad.

I can see only one difference in the gay countries; the Bible is little read and there is gallantry there. I apologize for lingering over the demonstration of something of which I am not sure. I am withholding twenty facts which bear out the foregoing.

97

In a fine castle near Paris I have just met a handsome, witty, wealthy young man of less than twenty; he chanced to be left almost alone there for a long time with an extremely beautiful girl of eighteen, talented, remarkably intelligent, and also very rich. Who would not have expected a passion to ensue? Nothing of the sort; both these pretty creatures were so eaten up with affectation that they were concerned only with themselves and with the effect they ought to produce upon each other.

98

I admit that from the moment of its great achievement this people has been led by a savage pride to commit all the errors and stupidities that opportunity offered. Here nevertheless is the reason why I cannot withdraw the words of praise I once uttered about this living counterpart of the Middle Ages.

The prettiest woman in Narbonne is a young Spanish girl, barely twenty, who lives in seclusion with her Spanish husband, an officer on half-pay. Some time ago the latter was obliged to slap the face of a certain coxcomb; the following day the coxcomb saw the young Spanish woman arrive at the place appointed for the duel; he burst out with a new torrent of affectation: 'But really, this is scandalous! How could you have admitted to your wife . . . I suppose Madame has come to prevent us fighting?' '*I have come to bury you*,' replied the young Spanish woman.

Happy the husband who can tell his wife everything. The result does not belie the loftiness of the pronouncement. Such an action would have been regarded in England as most improper. Thus false propriety diminishes what little happiness this world affords.

99

That charming fellow Donézan said yesterday: 'In my young days, and indeed until quite late in my life (for I was fifty in '89), women used to powder their hair.

'I confess to you that a woman without powder is repugnant to me and always gives me the impression of being a chambermaid who has had no time to finish her toilette.'

This is the only argument against Shakespeare and in favour of the unities.

Since young people read nothing but La Harpe, a liking for great powdered wigs like those worn by the late Queen Marie-Antoinette may persist for a few years yet. I also know some people who despise Correggio and Michael Angelo, and certainly M. Donézan is an extremely intelligent man.

100

Cold, brave, calculating, mistrustful, argumentative, always in fear of being stimulated by someone who might secretly be laughing at them, a little jealous of those who had witnessed great things under Napoleon, such were the young people of this period, more to be respected than to be liked. Naturally they brought the government round to a debased left-of-centre position. The characteristics of these young people were to be found even among conscripts, whose only ambition was to reach the end of their service.

All systems of education, whether intentionally or fortuitously administered, fit men for a particular period in their lives. Education in the time of Louis XV singled out twenty-five as the ideal age in its pupils.

The young people of this period will be at their best at forty, for they will have lost their mistrust and pretentiousness, and will have acquired gaiety and ease of manner.

IOI

Discussion between the man of good faith and the man from the Academy

'In this discussion with the academician, the latter always extricated himself by quibbling over minor dates or other similar trivial errors; but he persisted in denying, or pretended not to understand, the consequence and natural quiddity of things; for example that Nero had been a cruel emperor, or that Charles II had forsworn himself. Now how can such things be proved, or in proving them how can one avoid interrupting the main argument, and losing the thread of it?

'I have ever observed this kind of argument taking place between such people, where one is but seeking truth and yet more truth, while the other seeks the favour of his master or party and the glory of eloquence. And I hold it a great deception and waste of time for

the man of good faith to stop and talk with the afore-
said academicians.'

The Playful Works of Guy Allard de Voiron

102

Only a very small part of the art of being happy is
an exact science, a kind of ladder, up one rung of which
one is sure to climb every century; it is this part which
depends upon the government (and this is only a
theory; in my opinion the Venetians in 1707 were
happier than are the people of Philadelphia today).

Moreover, the art of being happy is like poetry;
despite the progress of all things towards perfection
Homer, two thousand seven hundred years ago, had
more talent than Lord Byron.

Reading Plutarch carefully I believe I can recognize
that even without the invention of printing and iced
punch they were happier in Sicily in the time of Dion
than we know how to be today.

I would rather be a fifth-century Arab than a nine-
teenth-century Frenchman.

103

It is never that illusion which renews and dispels
itself moment by moment which one goes to seek at
the theatre, but the opportunity of proving to one's
neighbour, or to oneself if one is so unlucky as to have
no neighbour, that one's La Harpe has been properly
conned and that one is a man of taste. This is a pleasure
fit for old pedants, in which youth is indulging.

104

A woman belongs by right to a man who loves her and whom she loves *more than life*.

105

Crystallization cannot be induced by men who imitate others, and the most dangerous rivals are those who are the most unorthodox.

106

In a highly civilized society *passionate love* is just as natural as physical love among savages.

Métilde

107

If it were not for the nuances, there would be no happiness in possessing a woman one adored; in fact it would be impossible.

L. 7th October

108

Whence comes the intolerance of the Stoics? From the same source as that of the bigotedly devout. They are ill-tempered because they are in conflict with Nature, because they deny themselves and because they suffer. If they could be brought honestly to analyse the hatred they bear towards those who profess a less rigid ethic, they would acknowledge that it derives from the concealed jealousy of a happiness they envy and have forbidden themselves to enjoy, *without believing* in the rewards that would repay their sacrifices.

Diderot

109

Habitually ill-tempered women might well ask themselves if they are following the code of behaviour which they *sincerely believe* to be the road to happiness. Is there not perhaps within the heart of a prude a certain lack of courage accompanied by a degree of mean vengefulness? Look at the ill-humour of Madame Deshoulières in her latter days.

Note by M. Lemontey

110

Nothing could be more indulgent, because nothing is happier, than sincere virtue; but Mistress Hutchinson herself lacks indulgence.

111

Next to this happiness comes that of a woman who is young, pretty, and easy-going, and who is not given to self-reproach. In Messina when they spoke ill of the Contessina Vicenzella she replied: 'What do you expect; I'm young, free, rich, and perhaps not ugly. I wish as much to all the women in Messina.' This delightful woman, who never felt more than friendship towards me, was the one who introduced me to the sweet poetry in Sicilian dialect by the Abbé Meli; lovely poems, though still spoilt by mythology.

Delfante

112

The Parisian public has a capacity for concentration which lasts for three days; beyond that limit, whether you offer them the death of Napoleon or M. Béranger sentenced to two months' imprisonment, the result is the same; and to speak of it on the fourth day betrays a similar lack of tact in the speaker. Is every great capital like this, or has it to do with the kindly superficiality of the Parisian? Thanks to aristocratic pride and painful self-consciousness London is nothing but a vast congregation of hermits and not a capital at all. Vienna is nothing but an oligarchy of two hundred families surrounded by a hundred and fifty thousand artisans and servants in their employ, and is no more a capital than London. Naples and Paris are the only two capitals.

Extract from Birkbeck's Travels, p. 371

113

If there were a period when, going by the commonplace theories regarded as reasonable by commonplace men, prison might be bearable, that period would be a month or two before the release of a poor prisoner detained for a number of years. But *crystallization* ordains otherwise. The last month is more painful than the three previous years. M. d'Hotelans has known several prisoners serving long sentences in Melun gaol who *died* of impatience only a few months before they were due to be freed.

114

I cannot resist the pleasure of quoting a letter written in poor English by a young German girl. Thus it is proved that constant love does exist, and that not every man of genius is a Mirabeau. The great poet Klopstock is reputed in Hamburg to have been a likeable man; here is what his young wife wrote to an intimate friend:

After having seen him two hours, I was obliged to pass the evening in a company, which never had been so wearisome to me. I could not speak, I could not play; I thought I saw nothing but Klopstock; I saw him the next day, and the following and we were very seriously friends. But the fourth day he departed. It was a strong hour the hour of his departure! He wrote soon after and from that time our correspondence began to be a very diligent one. I sincerely believed my love to be friendship. I spoke with my friends of nothing but Klopstock, and showed his letters. They raillied at me and said I was in love. I raillied then again, and said that they must have a very friendshipless heart, if they had no idea of friendship to a man as well as to a woman. Thus it continued eight months, in which time my friends found as much love in Klopstock's letters as in me. I perceived it likewise, but I would not believe it. At the last Klopstock said plainly that he loved; and I startled as for a wrong thing; I answered that it was no love, but friendship, as it was what I felt for him; we had not seen one another enough to love (as if love must have more time than friendship). This was sincerely my meaning, and I had this meaning till Klopstock came again to Hamburg. This he did a year after we had seen one another the first time. We saw, we were friends, we loved; and a short time after, I could even tell Klopstock that I loved. But we were obliged to part again, and wait two years for our wedding. My mother would not let marry me a stranger. I could marry then without her consentement, as by the death of my father my fortune depended not on her; but this was a horrible idea for me; and thank heaven that I have prevailed by prayers! At this time knowing Klopstock, she loves him as her lifely son, and thanks God that she has not persisted. We married and I am the happiest wife in the world. In some few months it will be four years that I am so happy . . .

Correspondence of Richardson, Vol. III, p. 147

115

The only unions which are legitimate for ever are those ruled by a genuine passion.

Métilde

116

To be happy in a lax moral climate a woman must have a simplicity of character such as one finds in Germany and Italy, but never in France.

The Duchesse de C—

117

The Turks in their pride deprive their wives of everything which might provide matter for crystallization.

For the last three months I have been living among a people whose titled folk, because of their pride, will soon have reached the same point.

The men give the name of *modesty* to the demands of a pride driven mad by aristocracy. How could one dare be found wanting in modesty? Also, as in Athens, intelligent men have a marked tendency to take refuge in the company of courtesans, that is to say women who through one outrageous mistake have found shelter from the affectations of *modesty*.

Life of Fox

118

Where love has been prevented by too early a victory, I have noticed that in sensitive people crystallization tries to set in afterwards. The woman says laughingly: 'No, I don't love you.'

119

The present system of education for women, that strange mixture of pious practices and lively songs (*di piacer mi balza il cor* from the *Gazza Ladra*), is the most effective way in the world to banish happiness. This education breeds the most illogical minds. Madame de R—, who feared death, has just died because she thought it was amusing to throw her medicine out of the window. These poor wretched women mistake inconsequence for gaiety, because gaiety is often apparently inconsequent. It is like the German who demonstrates his liveliness by throwing himself out of the window.

120

Vulgarity, by extinguishing imagination, has the immediate effect of boring me to death. The charming Countess K—, showing me her love-letters this evening, which I consider are coarse.

Forli, 17th March. Henri

Imagination had not been extinguished, but had merely lost its way, and from sheer distaste quickly gave up visualizing the coarseness of those dull lovers.

121

Metaphysical Reverie

Belgirate, 26th October 1816

Whenever a genuine passion encounters obstacles it probably produces more unhappiness than happiness; this idea may not hold good for a sensitive soul but is clearly true for the majority of men, and particularly for the cold philosophers who, in the sphere of passions, live almost entirely upon curiosity and self-esteem.

Yesterday evening, as we strolled along the terrace of the Isola Bella, on the east side, near the big pine, I related the foregoing to the Contessina Fulvia, who said to me: 'Unhappiness makes a much greater impression upon humanity than pleasure does.

'The most important quality of anything which claims to give us pleasure is that it should have a strong impact.

'Could one not conclude that, since life itself is entirely made up of sensations, the universal inclination of all living beings is towards awareness that their act of living depends on the strongest possible sensations? People from the North have little life; consider the slowness of their movements. The *dolce far niente* of the Italians is the pleasure of indulging in the emotions of the soul as one lies languidly upon a divan, a pleasure inconceivable to those who rush about all day on horseback or in a drosky like Englishmen or Russians. These people would die of boredom upon a divan. There is nothing in their souls for them to reflect upon.

'Love causes the strongest possible sensations; the proof of this is that in what physiologists would call moments of *inflammation* the heart forms those *associations of sensation* which seem so absurd to such philosophers as Helvétius and Buffon. The other day, as you know, Luizina fell into the lake; it was because she was watching a laurel leaf which had dropped into the water from a tree on the Isola Madre (Borromean Islands). The poor woman confessed to me that one day her lover, as he talked to her, was stripping the leaves from a laurel branch into the water, saying as he did so: "Your cruelties and the calumnies of your friend are denying me the enjoyment of life and the chance of glory."

'For some strange and quite incomprehensible reason, a soul which has known moments of anguish and intense unhappiness through the effects of some passion, ambition, gambling, love, jealousy, war, etc., *despises* the happiness of a peaceful life where everything seems made to order. A splendid castle in a picturesque situation, ample wealth, a good wife, three pretty children, numerous delightful friends: these are but a faint outline of all that our host General C— possesses, and yet you know he told us that he was tempted to go to Naples and take command of a guerilla band. A soul made for passion feels in the first place that this happy life *bores* him, and perhaps also that it only provides him with commonplace ideas. C— said to you: "I wish I had never known the fever of great passions, so that I might have profited by the apparent happiness about which I am paid such stupid compliments every day, and to which, as a crowning horror, I have to reply graciously."'

The philosopher in me rejoined: 'If you need a thousandth proof that we are not fashioned by a benign being, it is that *pleasure* produces only about half as much impression upon our being as *pain* does . . .'

The Contessina interrupted me: 'There are very few moral hardships in life which are not made more valuable by the *emotion* they excite; and if there is a fraction of generosity in the soul this pleasure is increased a hundredfold. A man condemned to death in 1815 and saved at the last moment (M. Lavalette for example), if he faced his torment bravely, must recall the occasion ten times a month; the coward who faces death sobbing and screaming (Morris the exciseman thrown into the lake; *Rob Roy* III, 120), if he too was saved at the last moment, can at best remember the occasion with pleasure only *because he was saved* and not because of any fund of generosity he discovered within himself, which rid the future of all its fears.'

Myself: 'Love, even unrequited love, provides a sensitive soul, for whom *what is imagined really exists*, with a fund of enjoyment of the same kind; sublime visions of happiness and beauty enwrap oneself and one's beloved. How often has Salviati not heard Léonore telling him, like Mademoiselle Mars in *Les Fausses Confidences*, with her bewitching smile, "Well, yes; I do love you!" Now these are illusions a prudent man never has.'

Fulvia (*raising her eyes to heaven*): 'Yes, for you and for me, love, even unrequited love, provided that our admiration of the beloved is infinite, is the greatest happiness of all.'

(Fulvia is twenty-three, and the most famous beauty in *****; her eyes were divine as she spoke, gazing up at the lovely midnight skies above the Borromean Islands; the very stars seemed to reply to her. I lowered my eyes, and could no longer find philosophical arguments to use against her). She continued: 'And all that the world calls happiness is not worth the trouble. I think only contempt can cure such a passion; not too great a contempt, for that would be torment; but for example, in the case of you men, to see the woman you adore loving a coarse and prosaic man, or giving you up for the sake of enjoying the trivial and dainty luxury she finds at the house of her friend.'

122

Will-power means the courage to run the risk of difficulty; to run such a risk means to tempt providence, to gamble. There are some soldiers who cannot exist without these gambles; this is what makes them quite unbearable in family life.

123

General Teulié told me this evening that he had discovered what made him so abominably taciturn and barren when there were affected women present in the drawing room. No sooner did he make a spirited exposition of his feelings in the presence of such creatures than he was smitten with bitter shame at having done so. (And if he did not speak from his heart, were it but of Punchinello, he had nothing to say. I noticed besides that he never knew the conventional or polite remark to make, and because of this he was always regarded as ridiculous and outlandish by affected women. Heaven had not created him to be elegant.)

124

At court irreligion is bad form because it is adjudged contrary to the interests of princes: it is also bad form in the presence of young girls, for it would prevent them from finding a husband. Doubtless, if God exists, he must find it pleasant to be honoured for motives such as these.

125

For a great painter or a great poet love is divine because it multiplies a hundredfold the scope and the pleasures of the art which gives his soul its daily bread. How many great artists there must be who never suspect the existence of their souls nor of their genius!

Often they believe themselves untalented for the thing they adore, because they are at variance with the eunuchs of the seraglio, or with people like La Harpe; for such artists even unhappy love means happiness.

126

The picture of first love is the most universally moving one; why? Because it is nearly always the same in all classes, in all countries, and in all characters. Therefore this first love is not the most passionate.

127

Be reasonable! Be reasonable! That is the cry invariably hurled at a poor lover. In 1760, at the climax of the Seven Years War, Grimm wrote: '. . . There is no doubt that the King of Prussia could have prevented this war before it broke out, by ceding Silesia. This would have been a very wise action on his part. How many evils he would have prevented! What could the mere possession of a province have to do with the happiness of a king? And was not the Great Elector a most contented and respected prince without possessing Silesia? That is how a king might have acted in accordance with the soundest precepts of reason, and I have no idea why such a king would have become the object of the whole world's contempt, while Frederick, in sacrificing everything to the *necessity* of holding Silesia, covered himself with immortal glory.

'Cromwell's son undoubtedly did the wisest thing a man could do, in preferring security and peace to the difficulty and danger of governing a sombre, fiery, and proud people. This wise man has been despised both in his lifetime and by posterity, while his father has remained a great man in the judgment of the nations.

'The Fair Penitent is a sublime theme from Spanish drama spoilt in English and French by Otway and Colardeau. Calista has been seduced by a man she adores, the impetuous pride of whose character makes him detestable, though his talents, wit, and grace, in fact all his qualities, combine to make him attractive. Lothario might have been only too engaging had he known how to moderate his infamous vehemence; besides this, a bitter hatred has for generations divided his family from that of the woman he loves. These two families are the leaders of two factions that rend a town in Spain during the horrors of the Middle Ages. Sciolto, Calista's father, is the chief of the opposing faction, which at that time is the stronger; he knows that Lothario has had the insolence to wish to seduce his daughter. The weak Calista succumbs, tortured by shame and passion. Her father succeeds in having his enemy appointed to the command of a long and dangerous naval expedition, on which Lothario will probably lose his life. In Colardeau's tragedy he tells his daughter of this, at which her passion bursts forth:

> *'Oh, ye Gods!*
> *He is going! On your orders! Has it then come to this?'*

'Consider the danger in this situation; one word more and Sciolto will know the truth of his daughter's passion for Lothario. The dumbfounded father cries out:

> *'Do my ears fail me? Whither strays your heart?'*

'At this Calista, who has come to her senses, replies:

> *"Not his mere exile but his death I seek;*
> *O let him perish!"*

'With these words Calista nips her father's suspicions in the bud, but quite artlessly, for the feeling she is expressing is real. The continued existence, even at the other end of the world, of a man whom she loves and who has been capable of outraging her, must poison her life; only his death could bring her peace, if peace there were for the lovelorn . . . Soon afterwards Lothario is killed, and Calista has the good fortune to die.

'"A great deal of weeping and gnashing of teeth over very little" has been the comment of those cold people who affect the name of philosophers. A bold and violent man takes advantage of a woman's weakness for him, but this is no cause for mourning, or at least is insufficient reason for us to take an interest in the woes of Calista. She has only to get over having slept with her lover, and will not be the first worthy woman to have resigned herself to that particular misfortune.'

Richard Cromwell, the King of Prussia, and Calista, with the souls that Heaven had given them, could only find tranquillity and happiness by acting in the way they did. The behaviour of the latter two is eminently un-reasonable, and yet they are the only ones to be respected.

Sagan. 1813

128

Constancy after happiness has been achieved can only be predicted in relation to that constancy which, despite cruel doubts, jealousy, and ridicule, existed before intimacy.

129

When a woman is in despair at the recent death of her lover on active service, and is obviously thinking of following him to the grave, one must first of all decide whether or not this would be a proper outcome. If the answer is negative, one must attack through that immemorial habit of humanity, her *instinct of self-preservation*. If the woman has an enemy, one can persuade her that this enemy has obtained a royal warrant for her summary imprisonment. If this threat does not increase her desire for death, she may begin to think of going into hiding to avoid incarceration. She should be in hiding for three weeks, fleeing from one refuge to another; she should be arrested, and escape three days later. Then under an assumed name she should be helped to find sanctuary in some very remote town as different as possible from the one where she was in despair. But who would wish to take up the cause of consoling so unhappy a being and one so unrewarding in friendship?

Warsaw. 1808

130

Academy scholars can see the customs of a people in its language: of all countries in the world Italy is the one where the word *love* is least used; it is always either *amicizia* or *avvicinar* (*amicizia* for love and *avvicinar* for courting crowned with success).

131

A dictionary of music has not yet been compiled nor even begun; it is only by chance that passages are found to express '*I am angry*' or '*I love you*' and their undertones. The composer only finds such passages when they are dictated to him by the presence of the particular passion in his heart, or by the recollection of it. Those young people who spend their ardent youth in study instead of in feeling can therefore never be artists – this whole mechanism is extremely simple.

132

The empire of women is much too extensive in France, and the empire of woman much too restricted.

133

The greatest flattery that the most frenzied imagination could invent, to describe the generation growing up amongst us to take possession of life, opinion, and power, turns out to be a truth clearer than daylight. The new generation has nothing to *continue* but everything to *create*. The great merit of Napoleon is that *he made a clean sweep*.

134

I should like to be able to say a few words about *consolation*. People make too little effort to be consoling.

The general principle is that one must be sure to develop a crystalization as far removed as possible from the cause of the suffering.

One must have the courage to engage in a little anatomy in order to discover an unknown principle.

If one cares to consult Chapter II of M. Villermé's work upon prisons (Paris, 1820), one will see that prisoners *si maritano fra di loro* (the phrase is prisoners' jargon). The women also *si maritano fra di loro*, and such unions are generally most faithful, which is not observed to be the case for men, and which is an effect of the principle of modesty.

'At Saint-Lazare,' M. Villermé writes on page 96, 'at Saint-Lazare in October 1818 a woman inflicted several knife-wounds upon herself because a newcomer was preferred to herself.

'It is normally the younger one who is the more attached to her partner.'

135

Vivacità, leggerezza soggettissima a prendere puntiglio, occupazione di ogni momenzo delle apparenze della propria esistenza agli occhi altrui: ecco i tre gran caratteri di questa pianta che risveglia Europa nell 1808.

The best among the Italians are those in whom a certain savagery and taste for blood persist; those of

Romagna and Calabria, and among the more civilized the Brescians, Piedmontese, and Corsicans.

The middle-class Florentine is even more of a sheep than his Parisian counterpart.

The espionage of Leopold has degraded him for ever. See M. Courrier's letter about Furia the librarian and Puccini the chamberlain.

136

I find it laughable to see men of goodwill always unable to agree, speaking ill of each other as a matter of course, and thinking worse. To live is to feel life and to experience strong sensations. Since the intensity of sensation differs according to the individual, what is too painfully strong for one man is precisely what another requires to arouse his interest. For example the sensation of coming unscathed through cannon-fire, or the sensation of chasing those Parthians into the depths of Russia; in the same way tragedy in Shakespeare and tragedy in Racine, etc., etc.

Orcha, 13th August 1812

137

In the first place, pleasure does not produce half as much impression as does pain, and in addition to this disadvantage of a lower emotional yield the picture of happiness excites at most only half as much *sympathy* as does the picture of misfortune. Hence poets can never be too powerful in their portrayal of unhappiness; they must beware only of one pitfall, themes which inspire disgust. Here again the *intensity* of this sensation depends upon the monarchy or the republic. The reign of a Louis XIV increases a hundredfold the number of repulsive themes (Poems of Crabbe).

Through the very fact of the existence of a monarchy like that of Louis XIV surrounded by his nobles, everything simple in the arts becomes coarse. The noble personage before whom the simplicity is displayed feels himself insulted, and this feeling is sincere and therefore to be respected.

Look what gentle Racine made of the heroic and time-honoured friendship between Orestes and Pylades. Orestes addresses Pylades in the second person singular, while Pylades replies to him as *my lord*. And we are expected to find Racine our most moving author! If an example such as this fails to convince, we had better change the subject.

138

As soon as one sees a hope of revenge, hatred breaks out afresh. Until my last few weeks in prison I had no thought of escaping or of breaking the oath I had sworn to my friend. Two admissions made tonight in my presence by a well-connected murderer who told us his whole story.

Faenza, 1817

139

The whole of Europe put together could not produce a single one of our good French books: *Les Lettres Persanes*, for instance.

140

I give the name of *pleasure* to anything which the soul would rather perceive than not perceive.

I give the name of *pain* to anything which the soul would rather not perceive than perceive.

If I wish to go to sleep rather than feel what I am feeling, then it is certainly *pain*. Therefore the desires of love are not pains, because the lover will forgo the most pleasant company in order to dream at his leisure.

The pleasures of the body are diminished by time while its pains are augmented thereby.

As for the pleasures of the soul, they are augmented or diminished by time according to the passions concerned; for example after six months spent in studying astronomy one likes astronomy better; after a year of avarice one prefers money.

The pains of the soul are diminished by time: 'How many genuinely heartbroken widows are consoled by the passage of time!' – Horace Walpole's Lady Waldegrave.

Suppose there is a man in a state of indifference, who experiences a pleasure.

Suppose there is another man in a state of acute pain, which ceases abruptly. Is the pleasure felt by the second of the same quality as that of the first man? M. Verri thinks it is, and I do not.

Not all pleasures are the result of the cessation of pain.

For a long time a man has had an income of six thousand francs a year; he wins five hundred thousand francs in a lottery. This man has lost the habit of desiring those things which only great wealth can afford. (I might say in passing that one of the inconvenient things about Paris is the ease with which this habit can be lost.)

The quill-sharpener has now been invented; I bought one this morning, and it is a great pleasure to me, for I grow impatient at sharpening my pens; but certainly I was not unhappy yesterday for not knowing about this machine. Do you suppose Petrarch was unhappy because he never drank coffee?

It is useless to define happiness, for everyone knows what it is: for example one's first partridge brought down on the wing at twelve; the first battle from which one emerges safe and sound at seventeen.

Pleasure which is merely the cessation of a pain is soon over, and after a few years even the memory of it is no longer agreeable. A friend of mine was wounded in the side by a shell at the battle of the Moskova; some days later he was threatened with gangrene, and within a few hours M. Béclar, M. Larrey, and several renowned surgeons were together in consultation, and the result was that my friend was informed that he did not have gangrene. In that instant I saw his happiness, which was great, and yet not unmixed. Secretly in his own mind he did not feel quite free of it, and went over the work the surgeons had done, deliberating whether he could entirely rely on them. The possibility of gangrene still hovered before his eyes. Today, eight years afterwards, when this consultation is mentioned to him he experiences a feeling of pain, at the unexpected vision of one of the misfortunes of life.

The pleasure caused by the cessation of pain consists in:

1. winning a victory over all one's successive misgivings;
2. reviewing all the advantages one was about to lose.

The pleasure caused by the acquisition of five hundred thousand francs consists in anticipating all the new and extraordinary pleasures in which one is going to indulge.

There is one singular exception: we must determine whether this man is too much or too little in the habit of desiring a great fortune. If he is too little in this habit, if he is small-minded, the feeling of encumbrance will last two or three days.

If he is often in the habit of desiring a great fortune he will have used up the enjoyment of it in imagination beforehand.

This misfortune does not occur in passionate love.

A burning soul does not imagine the ultimate favour, but the nearest one. For example, with a mistress who treats you severely you dream of holding her hand. Imagination does not naturally reach beyond the first step, and if it is forced it will very soon retreat for fear of profaning what it adores.

When pleasure has entirely run its course it is clear that one sinks back into indifference, but an indifference which is not the same as before. This second state differs from the first in that it appears we are no longer able to take such delight in enjoying the pleasure we have just experienced.

The organs employed in feeling it are tired, and the imagination is no longer so capable of presenting images attractive to desires which are now satisfied.

But if in the midst of pleasure we are wrenched away from it, suffering will result.

141

The disposition to physical love and even to physical pleasure is not at all the same for the two sexes. Unlike men, nearly all women are at least susceptible to one kind of love. From the very first novel a woman opens surreptitiously at fifteen she awaits in secret the advent of passionate love. She sees a grand passion as proof of her merit. This anticipation is intensified at about the age of twenty, when she has outgrown her early blunders; whereas men no sooner reach the age of thirty than they believe love is impossible or absurd.

142

From the age of six we become accustomed to seek happiness along the same paths as our parents. The unhappiness of the charming Contessina Nella derives from the pride of her mother, and she perpetuates it with the same mad pride.

Venice, 1819

143

On the Romantic Style

I am told in a letter from Paris that they have just seen a thousand or so pictures (Exhibition of 1822) representing scenes from the Holy Scriptures, painted by painters who have little belief in them, admired and judged by people who don't believe in them, and then bought by people who don't believe in them either.

And yet we seek a reason for the decadence of art.

With no belief in what he is expressing, the artist is always afraid lest he appear exaggerated and absurd. How can he attain the *grandiose* when nothing lifts him towards it?

Lettera di Roma, Giugno, 1822

144

In my opinion one of the greatest poets in these latter days is Robert Burns, a Scottish peasant who died of poverty. As an excise agent he had a wage of seventy louis for himself, his wife, and four children. It must be agreed, for example, that the tyrant Napoleon was more generous to his enemy Chénier. Burns had none of the prudishness of the English. His was a latin genius bereft of chivalry and honour. Space does not permit me to relate the story of his love 'for Mary Campbell, which culminated in mournful catastrophe. But I notice that Edinburgh is in the same latitude as Moscow, which may to some extent upset my system of climates.

'One of Burns' remarks, when he first came to Edinburgh, was that between the men of rustic life and the polite world he observed little difference, that in the former, though unpolished by fashion and unenlightened by science, he had found much observation and much intelligence; but a refined and accomplished woman was a being almost new to him, and of which he had formed but a very inadequate idea.'

London, 1st November 1821, Vol. V, p. 69

145

Love is the only passion which rewards itself in a coin of its own manufacture.

146

The compliments paid to little girls of three constitute the best possible form of education for teaching them the most pernicious vanity. To be pretty is chief among the virtues, and the greatest advantage there is. To have a pretty dress is to be pretty.

These stupid compliments are only current among the bourgeoisie; fortunately among those who own carriages they are considered bad form, as being too facile.

147

Loretto, 11th September 1811

I have just seen a very fine battalion of the men of this region; they are all that remain of four thousand men who went to Vienna in 1809. I walked through the ranks with their colonel, and at my request several soldiers told me their stories. Here is the virtue of the medieval republics, more or less debased by the Spaniards, the priesthood, and two centuries of cowardly and cruel governments who have each in their turn spoilt this land.

Brilliant chivalric *honour*, sublime and irrational,

is an exotic plant imported only within fairly recent years.

There is no sign of it in 1740. See de Brosses. The officers of Montenotte and Rivoli too often had occasion to display genuine virtue to their neighbours for them to seek to *imitate* an honour little known within the cottage homes of the soldiers of 1796, and one which would have seemed very strange to them.

In 1796 there was neither a Legion of Honour nor enthusiasm for any one man, but a great deal of simplicity and virtue in the manner of Desaix. Hence *honour* was imported into Italy by people too rational and too virtuous to be really brilliant. One feels it is a far cry from the soldiers of '96 winning twenty battles in a year, and often without shoes or uniform, to the brilliant regiments at Fontenoy, doffing their hats and saying politely to the English: 'Will you fire first, gentlemen?'

148

I am prepared to believe that the goodness of a way of life must be judged through its representatives. For instance Richard Cœur-de-Lion on his throne appeared to be a paragon of heroism and valorous chivalry, though he was really a ridiculous king.

149

Public opinion in 1822. A man of thirty seduces a girl of fifteen, and it is the girl who is dishonoured.

150

Ten years later I met Countess Ottavia again; she wept copiously at seeing me again; I reminded her of Oginski. 'I can no longer love,' she told me; I answered her in the words of the poet: 'How changed, how saddened, yet how elevated was her character!'

151

Just as the English way of life came into existence between 1688 and 1730, that of France will be created between 1815 and 1880. Nothing will be so beautiful, just, or happy as the moral atmosphere of France in about 1900. At present it is none of these. What is infamous in the Rue de Belle-Chasse is heroic in the Rue du Mont-Blanc, and in the midst of all the exaggerations, people genuinely worthy of contempt escape by moving into the next street. We had one recourse, the freedom of the press, which in the end tells all and sundry the truth about themselves, and if this truth happens to coincide with public opinion it endures. This safeguard is now being wrested from us, which will somewhat delay the advent of morality.

152

The Abbé Rousseau was a poor young man (1784) reduced to chasing about all over the city from morning to night giving history and geography lessons. In love with one of his pupils, like Abelard with Héloïse, like Saint-Preux with Julie; less happy, certainly, but probably very near to being so; with as much passion as the latter, but more honest, more fastidious, and above all more courageous, he appears to have sacrificed himself to the object of his passion. Here is what he wrote before he blew out his brains, after having dined at a restaurant near the Palais-Royal where he betrayed no sign of anxiety or insanity; the text of the note is taken from the investigation report drawn up on the spot by the police inspector and his officers, and is sufficiently remarkable to merit preservation.

'The inexpressible contrast which exists between the nobility of my feelings and the meanness of my birth, my love for an adorable girl, as violent as it is insuperable, the fear of being the agent of her dishonour, the necessity of choosing between crime and death, all these have made me resolve to abandon life. I was born to be virtuous, I was about to be criminal; I preferred to die.'

Grimm, Third Part, Vol. II, p. 495

This is a suicide worthy of admiration, and one which would be simply absurd in the moral climate of 1880.

153

In the fine arts, however hard they try, the French will never transcend the *pretty*.

Comedy requiring a *spirited* audience and actors with *brio*, the delightful jokes of Palomba played by Casaccia at Naples, impossible in Paris; prettiness and ever more prettiness, though sometimes, it is true, announced as sublime.

The reader will note that I am not in the habit of speculating about national honour.

154

'We like a beautiful picture very much,' say the French, and they are quite right; but we make it an essential condition of beauty that it should have been executed by a painter who stands on one leg whenever he is working. Verse in dramatic art.

155

Far less *envy* in America than in France, and far less wit.

156

Tyranny in the manner of Philip II has so degraded men's minds since 1530 that it has cast its shadow over the garden of the world, so that the poor Italian authors have not yet had the courage to *invent* their own national novel. Nevertheless, in view of the rule that everything must be *natural*, nothing could be simpler; they must have the courage to copy quite openly what stares them in the face in society. Look at Cardinal Conzalvi in 1822, gravely thumbing over the libretto of a comic opera for three hours, and saying anxiously to the composer: 'But you will often repeat this word *cozzar, cozzar.*'

157

Héloïse speaks to you of love, and some ass speaks to you of his love; don't you sense that these two things have nothing but the word in common? They are like a love of concerts and a love of music. Love of the delights of vanity offered you by your harp in the midst of dazzling society, or love of a tender, solitary, unassuming reverie.

158

When one has just seen the woman one loves, the sight of every other woman damages the vision and physically hurts the eyes; I can see why.

159

Answer to an objection.
Perfectly natural behaviour and intimacy can exist only in passionate love, for in every other kind one is aware that a rival may be favoured.

160

In a man who has taken poison to release himself from life the moral being is dead; stunned by what it has done and what it must experience it pays no further attention to anything; some rare exceptions.

161

An old sea-captain, the author's uncle, to whom I dedicate the present manuscript, thinks that nothing could be more ridiculous than to devote six hundred pages to anything as frivolous as love. This frivolous thing is nevertheless the only weapon with which one can assail strength of soul.

What stopped M. de Maubreuil from sacrificing

Napoleon in the forest of Fontainebleau in 1814? The contemptuous glance of a pretty woman entering the Chinese Baths. What a difference it would have made to the destiny of the world if Napoleon and his son had been killed in 1814!

162

I quote the following lines from a letter I received from Znaim written in French, and would add that in the whole province there is not a single man fit to understand the intelligent woman who wrote it to me.

'. . . chance plays a great part in love. When I have not read English for a year, I am delighted by the first novel I happen to pick up. The habit of loving a prosaic soul, that is to say one which is slow and shy towards anything delicate and which only feels passion for the coarser pursuits of life – love of gold, pride in fine horses, physical desires, etc. – may easily lead a person to regard as offensive the actions of a burning and impetuous genius with an impatient imagination, one who feels nothing but love and forgets all else, and who is continuously engaging in impetuous action in situations where the other lacked initiative and never acted of his own accord. The surprise such a genius arouses may offend what we called feminine pride (last year at Zithau); is this a French concept? To the second, the reaction is one of *surprise*, a feeling unknown in relation to the first (and as the first died unexpectedly in the army he has remained a synonym for perfection); a feeling moreover which a soul full of dignity, and lacking that ease of manner which stems from the experience of several love affairs, can easily confuse with what is offensive.'

163

Geoffroy Rudel of Blaye was a very great nobleman, prince of Blaye, and he became enamoured of the Countess of Tripoli, though he had not seen her, by reason of the great good and the great courtesy he heard tell of her from the pilgrims coming from Antioch; he made many beautiful songs for her with good melodies and weak words; and wishing to see her he crossed himself and embarked on the sea to go to her. And it happened that on the ship he was stricken with a grievous sickness, so that those who were with him believed him dead, but went so far as to take him to an inn at Tripoli, as a dead man. The Countess being told of this, she came to his bedside and took him in her arms. He knew that she was the Countess and recovered his sight and his hearing, and praised God, and thanked Him for having spared his life until he had seen her. And thus he died in the arms of the Countess, who had him honourably buried in the House of the Temple at Tripoli. And that same day she took the veil of a nun, because of her grief for him and for his death.

164

Here is a curious proof of the madness called crystallization, taken from the *Memoirs* of Mistress Hutchinson:

'. . . He told to Mr Hutchinson a very true story of

a gentleman who not long before had come for some time to lodge in Richmond, and found all the people he came in company with, bewailing the death of a gentlewoman that had lived there. Hearing her so much deplored he made enquiry after her, and grew so in love with the description, that no other discourse could at first please him, nor could he at last endure any other; he grew desperately melancholy, and would go to a mount where the print of her foot was cut, and lie there pining and kissing of it all the day long, till at length death in some months space concluded his languishment. This story was very true.'

Vol. I, p. 83

165

Lisio Visconti was nothing if not a great reader of books. Besides what he had been able to observe as he went about the world this essay is also based upon the memoirs of fifteen or twenty famous people. In case one of its readers should perchance consider these trifles worthy of a moment's attention, here are the books from which Lisio drew his reflections and conclusions:

Life of Benvenuto Cellini, by himself.

The *Short Stories* of Cervantes and Scarron.

Manon Lescaut and *Le Doyen de Killerine* by the Abbé Prevôt.

The Latin Letters of Héloïse to Abélard.

Tom Jones.

Letters of a Portuguese Nun.

Two or three novels by Auguste La Fontaine.

History of Tuscany by Pignotti.
Werther.
Brantôme.
Memoirs of Carlo Gozzi (Venice, 1760); only the 80 pages dealing with the story of his loves.
Memoirs of Lauzun, Saint-Simon, d'Epinay, de Staal, Marmontel, Bezanval, Roland, Duclos, Horace Walpole, Evelyn, Hutchinson.
Letters of Mademoiselle Lespinasse.

166

One of the greatest figures of the time, one of the most outstanding men in Church and State, told us at the home of Mme de M— this evening (January 1822) about the very real dangers he had run during the Terror.

'I had the misfortune to be one of the best-known members of the Constituent Assembly; I stayed in Paris, trying with indifferent success to hide myself, as long as there was some hope that the cause of right would triumph. At length, as the tide of danger was rising and the foreigners did nothing energetic to help us, I made up my mind to leave, but it had to be done without a passport. Since everybody seemed to be making for Coblenz I thought I should try to make my exit through Calais. But my portrait had been so widely circulated eighteen months earlier that I was recognized at the last staging-post, though they let me pass. I reached an inn at Calais where, as you may imagine, I scarcely slept a wink, and this was extremely lucky because at about four in the morning I heard my name spoken distinctly. As I rose and dressed in haste I could see, despite the darkness, national guards with their muskets, coming into the courtyard of the inn through the main gate which had been opened for them. Fortunately it was pouring with rain and a very dark and windy winter morning. The darkness and the noise of the wind enabled me to escape through the back yard and the stables, and there I was in the street at seven in the morning, with no resources whatever.

'I assumed that my pursuers would follow me from the inn, and with no very clear idea what I was doing I made my way to the port and on the jetty. I admit that I had to some extent lost my head, and could see nothing but the prospect of the guillotine.

'There was a packet putting out from the port in a heavy sea, and already twenty fathoms from the jetty. All at once I heard shouts from the direction of the sea, as if I were being hailed. I saw a small boat coming up. "Come along, Sir. You're expected." Mechanically I stepped aboard the boat, in which was a man who whispered to me: "When I saw you walk on to the jetty looking so frantic I thought you might well be an unfortunate outlaw. I said you were a friend I was expecting; you must pretend to be seasick and hide yourself below in a dark corner of the cabin."'

'Oh, what a magnificent gesture!' cried the lady of the house breathlessly, moved to tears by the long and well-told recital of the Abbé's dangers. 'How you must have thanked this generous stranger! What was his name?'

'I do not know his name,' replied the Abbé in some

confusion; and there was a moment of dead silence in the drawing-room.

167

Father and Son
A dialogue of 1787

The father, (*Minister for War*):

'I congratulate you, my boy; it's a very pleasant thing for you to have been invited to M. le duc d'Orléans. It's an honour for a man of your age. Make sure you are at the Palais-Royal at six o'clock precisely.'

The son:

'I believe, sir, that you are to dine there as well?'

The father:

'M. le duc d'Orléans, who has always been most good to our family, has been kind enough to invite me as well, as he is requesting your presence for the first time.'

The son, a well-born young man of most distinguished intelligence, was at the Palais-Royal without fail at six o'clock. Dinner was served at seven. The son found himself sitting opposite his father. Each guest had a naked girl sitting beside him. Twenty footmen in full livery were serving.

168

London, August 1817

Never in my life have I been so struck and overawed by the presence of beauty as I was this evening at a concert given by Mme Pasta.

She was surrounded as she sang by three rows of young women so lovely, so pure and celestial in their beauty, that I felt myself lower my eyes respectfully instead of raising them to admire and enjoy. I have never felt the like in any country, not even in my beloved Italy.

169

If there is one thing utterly out of the question in the arts in France it is verve. For a man to be enthusiastic would be too ridiculous; *he would look too happy*. But see a Venetian reciting Buratti's satires.

170

In Valencia in Spain there lived two friends, very respectable women belonging to distinguished families. One of them was courted by a French officer who loved her passionately, even to the point of forgoing his medal after a battle because he stayed with her in his billet instead of going to headquarters to curry favour with the general in command.

In the end she came to love him. After seven months of coldness as heartbreaking at the end as it was in the beginning, she said to him one evening: 'Dear Joseph, I am yours.' There remained an obstacle in the shape of a husband, an extremely intelligent but excessively jealous man. In my capacity of friend I had to read through with the husband the whole of Rulhière's History of Poland, which he did not understand very well. Three months went by without our having been able to deceive him. Telegraph messages were sent on feast days to indicate which church they would attend for mass.

One day I noticed that my friend was more depressed than usual; here is what was going to happen. Dona Inezilla's friend was dangerously ill, and she asked her husband's permission to go and spend the night with the invalid. This was agreed immediately on condition that the husband should choose the day. One evening he took Dona Inezilla round to her friend's house, and apparently on the spur of the moment said playfully that he would sleep very well on a sofa in a little drawing-room which gave into the bedroom, and of which the door was left open. For eleven days the French officer spent two hours every evening hidden under the invalid's bed. I dare not add the sequel.

I do not think vanity would permit a Frenchwoman to exhibit this degree of friendship.

THE STORY OF PENGUIN CLASSICS

Before 1946 ...'Classics' are mainly the domain of academics and students, without readable editions for everyone else. This all changes when a little-known classicist, E. V. Rieu, presents Penguin founder Allen Lane with the translation of Homer's Odyssey that he has been working on and reading to his wife Nelly in his spare time.

1946 The Odyssey becomes the first Penguin Classic published, and promptly sells three million copies. Suddenly, classic books are no longer for the privileged few.

1950s Rieu, now series editor, turns to professional writers for the best modern, readable translations, including Dorothy L. Sayers's *Inferno* and Robert Graves's *The Twelve Caesars*, which revives the salacious original.

1960s 1961 sees the arrival of the Penguin Modern Classics, showcasing the best twentieth-century writers from around the world. Rieu retires in 1964, hailing the Penguin Classics list as 'the greatest educative force of the 20th century'.

1970s A new generation of translators arrives to swell the Penguin Classics ranks, and the list grows to encompass more philosophy, religion, science, history and politics.

1980s The Penguin American Library joins the Classics stable, with titles such as *The Last of the Mohicans* safeguarded. Penguin Classics now offers the most comprehensive library of world literature available.

1990s Penguin Popular Classics are launched, offering readers budget editions of the greatest works of literature. Penguin Audiobooks brings the classics to a listening audience for the first time, and in 1999 the launch of the Penguin Classics website takes them online to an ever larger global readership.

The 21st Century Penguin Classics are rejacketed for the first time in nearly twenty years. This world famous series now consists of more than 1,300 titles, making the widest range of the best books ever written available to millions – and constantly redefining the meaning of what makes a 'classic'.

The Odyssey continues ...

The best books ever written

PENGUIN CLASSICS

SINCE 1946

Find out more at www.penguinclassics.com